Anne Karpf is a writer, medical sociologist and award-winning journalist. She has been a contributing editor to *Cosmopolitan*, and wrote a weekly column for the family pages of the *Guardian*, to which she now contributes columns on social, political and cultural issues. She also writes for the *Independent on Sunday* and other publications. A regular broadcaster, she writes and presents for BBC Radio 4, and is the author of three books, including *The Human Voice* (Bloomsbury, 2007). She is Reader in Professional Writing and Cultural Inquiry at London Metropolitan University.

The School of Life is dedicated to exploring life's big questions: *How do we find fulfilling work? Can we ever understand our past? Why are relationships so hard to master? If we could change the world, should we?* Based in London, with offices around the globe, The School of Life offers classes, therapies, books and other tools to help you create a more satisfying life. We don't have all the answers but we will direct you towards a variety of ideas from the humanities

from philosophy to literature, psychology to the visual arts – guaranteed to stimulate, provoke, nourish and console.

How to Age
Anne Karpf

MACMILLAN

First published 2014 by Macmillan
an imprint of Pan Macmillan, a division of
Macmillan Publishers Limited

Pan Macmillan
20 New Wharf Road, London N1 9RR
Basingstoke and Oxford
Associated companies throughout the world
www.panmacmillan.com

ISBN 978-0-230-76775-1

9 8 7 6 5 4 3 2 1

A CIP catalogue record for this book is
available from the British Library.

Cover design by Marcia Mihotich
Typeset by seagulls.net
Printed and bound by CPI Group (UK) Ltd,
Croydon, CR0 4YY

Visit **www.panmacmillan.com** to
read more about all our books and to
buy them. You will also find features,
author interviews and news of any
author events, and you can sign up for
e-newsletters so that you're always first
to hear about our new releases.

For Peter

'Oh God! May I be alive when I die'
– Donald Winnicott

Contents

Introduction

It's the morning of Gina's thirtieth birthday, as her follicles helpfully remind her: she finds her second grey hair. At work, two birthday cards are propped up on her desk. The first says 'There's no need to torture yourself just because you're turning 30 . . . life will do that for you!' The second has no words, simply a reproduction of Edvard Munch's *The Scream* with the number 30 superimposed.

Gina's boyfriend, Jack, is of little comfort. On his fortieth birthday a month earlier, the card from his best mate read 'You're 40?! Well, you're still young enough to live a little . . . but hurry!', while his brother's bore the message 'Happy Birthday . . . and cheer up! In time you'll learn to love being 40 . . . like in ten years when you're turning 50!'

Neither Gina nor Jack have told their friends or family how uncomfortable these cards make them feel: they know it would only provoke those mantras of the passive-aggressive: 'Where's your sense of humour?' and 'Can't you take a joke?' But you don't need to have read Freud's *Jokes and Their Relation to the Unconscious* (though if you haven't, do – it's packed with good jokes) to know that humour is a way that we articulate and manage anxiety.

Gina's parents are no help either. Her 56-year-old mother, Sara, in between her Pilates class and collagen-implant appointment, is packing for a weekend at a spa, while her 62-year-old father, Clive, is going off on a jet-skiing trip, after attending a public lecture by the author of 'Generation Ageless'.

Though Gina's parents might seem to have vaporized any anxieties about ageing – having lasered them away, along with their forehead furrows – in fact both Gina and Jack and her parents are suffering from the same, painful condition: a deep fear of ageing.

If the demographic predictions are correct, Gina and Jack may well live until they're 100: this means that they're going to be worried for an awfully long time. Gina's parents, however, are convinced that, as baby boomers, they have extirpated ageing, her dad insisting – like Mick Jagger – that his crow's feet are simply laughter lines. (He clearly never heard the writer and musician George Melly's riposte to Jagger: 'Nothing's that funny'.)

Both generations of this family monitor their body for any signs of ageing: Gina's mother compares herself favourably to those people shamed on a website listing Which Celebrities Haven't Aged Well, while Gina is nervous that her birthday marks the start of an inexorable process of decline. The parents deny the fact that they're getting older; the daughter dreads it.

A third approach to ageing

But this family hasn't dreamed up these punitive narratives all by itself: they are historically determined and culturally shaped. And even in Western cultures today there is a third way of viewing the ageing process, one which starts by questioning the very idea of old age as a homogenous entity – a planet Old, of which one automatically becomes a citizen on one's fiftieth or sixtieth birthday, or, if you're a pessimist, a decade or two earlier.

How absurd of us to envisage 40- or 50- or 60- to 100-year-olds as a single cohort – no less ridiculous than conceiving of the ages of 0 to 40 in such a way! Ah, you might protest, but those first four decades are ones of immense change. And here we smoke out one of the most entrenched prejudices about ageing – that it's a time of stagnation. Or, if not stagnation, then the change is all in one direction: that of decline. In fact, as we'll see, ageing can be actively enriching, a time of immense growth. Perhaps that's why it's called 'growing old'.

What's more, on one thing all the leading researchers concur: that we become more, and not less, diverse as we age. Age doesn't obliterate our individual traits and identities – on the contrary, it heightens them. In truth there are far more differences among individuals *within* the same age-group than there are *between* age-groups: a middle-class, white, healthy, male 72-year-old Londoner probably has more in common with a middle-class, white, healthy, male 32-year-old Londoner than with a black, undernourished, female, rural 72-year-old Ecuadorian with eight children and who cares for four grandchildren. And neither of them may see their age as their most significant characteristic. (Indeed income, race and social class are probably far more formative.)

This might surprise Gina, who thinks that, on receipt of her free bus pass, she'll become nothing but old – all her other characteristics, idiosyncrasies and personal history erased or subsumed beneath that asphyxiating carapace of OLD, which has already begun to cast its shadow over her 30-year-old life. Who wouldn't be scared?

If age is everything for Gina, it's nothing for her mother, who refuses to make any concessions to her age, as though the merest whiff of recognition of the process might somehow, magically, accelerate it. She therefore condemns herself to expending vast amounts of energy in fighting ageing, energy that she might have devoted to living more richly.

But the third approach to age, mapped out in this book, is far more affirming and engaging. It sees ageing as a lifelong process, not something confined to its latter stages, and an opportunity to develop – indeed an intrinsic part of life itself. In order to start down this path we have to break the taboo against ageing, and acknowledge that growing older is inevitable – if we're lucky. A long life signals that we're privileged, either through genetic serendipity, affluence or sheer luck. Woody Allen insisted that he had nothing against growing older 'since nobody had found a better way of not dying young.'

This acknowledgement of ageing involves mourning, because there are inevitable losses associated with getting older, whether in function (no 50-year-old is ever going to win Wimbledon, and even turning 35 probably puts you out of contention), or the death of friends and family, or the recognition of one's own mortality. But while mourning is painful – it means tolerating sadness – the idea that ageing is nothing but a trajectory of decline is bewilderingly misleading.

The gains of age

Indeed, once we rid ourselves of the 'deficit' model of ageing, it becomes apparent that nature is often more even-handed than

Frank Lloyd Wright completed the design of his masterpiece, the Solomon R. Guggenheim Museum in New York, when he was 80.

we've supposed: recent neurological research shows that the brain in midlife – roughly 35 to 65 and even beyond – is far more elastic than most of us had realized. Short-term memory may decline but we make better connections between what we retain. Winston Churchill became prime minister at 66, and architect Frank Lloyd Wright completed the design of his masterpiece, the Solomon Guggenheim Museum in New York, when he was 80.

World history is full of late developers – not necessarily exceptional individuals notching up record-breaking achievements, but ordinary ones who've found fresh ways of developing new capacities and relationships, who understand that we can continue to grow so long as we continue to breathe, and that some aspects of the self, like spiritual growth, take time. Indeed for many of us this kind of growth is one of the unexpected rewards of ageing, and it can start to develop even when we're young adults. In the research for this book I've interviewed people of all ages. What's striking is how almost all of them felt enlarged and not diminished by ageing.

Ageing, if we allow it to, supplies us with a constantly shifting panorama, something that the caricatures of age obscure or simplify. For example we aren't simply children and then adults: relations with parents and the struggle to separate can continue to be fraught into one's twenties and well beyond. And yet English has no ungendered word for the adult offspring. It's as if we have no conception of the parent–child bond enduring beyond childhood, and so no need for a word beyond 'adult children', a term that sounds like an oxymoron.

Despite this book's title, which is intended to challenge the notion that the only good way of ageing is not to, it can't supply a recipe or prescription; on the contrary, this book develops from the belief that we need to free ourselves from prescriptive ideas of how an older, or indeed a younger, person should look, sound or live. The psychoanalyst Donald Winnicott said that living creatively involves retaining something personal that is unmistakably yourself. The view of ageing that this book encourages and reflects, while never pretending away some of the indignities and challenges of old age, sees the continuities between our younger and older selves: we remain ourselves throughout the life cycle, only older. Even more importantly, ageing offers us the opportunity – one identified by the writer May Sarton in her luminous journal *At Seventy*, which chronicled the year that began on her seventieth birthday – of becoming more fully ourselves: more, and not less, individual. Ageing, at each stage of life, can be actively enriching.

If Gina moves beyond her fear, she'll realize that this has already started to happen to her: that she is, in fact, more satisfied with her life at 30 than she was at 20 – she understands herself better, her relationships are more solid. Gina's fear of ageing is directed at some amorphous, creeping, malign change, which prevents her from appreciating the benefits that she has already derived from the ageing process. It's as if there's a cognitive dissonance at work, leading Gina to hold two contradictory attitudes simultaneously: she's scared of what has already, quite benignly, begun to take place. She's ageing with vitality, even while she fears getting older.

Winnicott also maintained that creative living resulted in surprising oneself. The capacity to be surprised, curious and engaged isn't the prerogative of young people (we should refuse the term 'the young' just as forcefully as we refuse to speak of 'the old' – it's part of resisting the homogenizing tendency), and indeed it can intensify as we age.

Greeting the ageing self

In trying to depathologize age, we need to make an important distinction, between resisting ageism (stereotyping or discriminating on the basis of age) and resisting age itself. The first opens the door to a path of rich potential, freeing us to keep on developing and changing, while the second closes it, condemning us to an endless attempt to recover the irretrievable.

We need also to understand how, as the writer Margaret Morganroth Gullette put it, we are 'aged by culture'. In Western societies we tend to think of ageing in biomedical terms, as a physiological condition. And of course we are embodied creatures, the state of our bodies as we age making certain activities possible and closing off others. But an equally, if not more, crucial factor shaping the way that we age is the culture in which we live: not only its attitude towards ageing, but also its policies. For swathes of people, getting older means getting poorer, which in turn leads to them being marginalized from the pleasures and plenitude of life. The more noisily we promote the third approach to ageing, one which embraces ageing and sees it as a lifelong process, the more apparent it will become that poverty isn't intrinsic to ageing but results from policies and practices expressing contempt and indifference to older people and to the ageing process itself – and that can be resisted by all of us, whatever our age.

In the chapters that follow, I introduce the idea of ageing as a lifelong process, one to be celebrated, and then spell out the fear of ageing, embodied by Gina and her parents, that so saturates our thinking. Having explored this, I offer revivifying examples of people embracing ageing, and consider how we might follow in their footsteps. Next, I chart historical and cultural changes in attitudes to ageing, and show how age-apartheid is being challenged. I dedicate a separate chapter to exploring the ways in which our experiences of ageing are gendered, and the recent extension of self-scrutiny to men. This is followed by a chapter that argues, in the words of Rabbi Zalman Schachter-Shalomi, that 'death is not a cosmic mistake' and that, if we work towards integrating it into our understanding of life from a very early age, it can paradoxically reduce the fear of ageing. Death then becomes part of what I call in the final chapter 'the arc of life', which allows us to connect our life experiences into a meaningful chain.

'Age takes hold of us by surprise,' remarked Goethe. Simone de Beauvoir couldn't believe it when she first stood in front of her mirror and said 'I am forty'. Gloria Steinem noted that 'One day I woke up and there was a 70-year-old woman in my bed.' (Interesting how much less quoted this is than her retort, upon being told by a reporter that she didn't look 40, 'This is what 40 looks like.') So caricatured and disavowed is the ageing process that older people regularly say, in amazement, 'I don't feel old – I still feel 18 inside.' They *are* still 18 inside – and 8, and 28, 38, 48 and 58: all those former ages aren't eviscerated by age but are enfolded inside them, like the rings in a tree trunk. The realization that, as we age, we don't have to be evicted from our predilections and passions, interests and senses – indeed from our bodies, whatever physical limitations we might experience; that we aren't catapulted into a homogenous category called old from which all traces of our prior identity have been expunged; that the zest for life can survive the inevitable curtailments and bereavements we suffer along the way – all this, surely, makes ageing a much less terrifying business.

Maggie Kuhn, founder of the American Gray Panther movement, an intergenerational, anti-ageist campaigning group, sympathized with Gina's unhappiness over leaving behind her twenties. Kuhn's thirtieth birthday had been her worst, she recalled – when she was 85.

Kuhn's thirtieth birthday had been her worst, she recalled – when she was 85.

1. What is Age?

Wrinkles, sensible shoes and Alzheimer's – these, or something like them, are what most of us would come up with if we were asked to free-associate on the subject of age. But they're utterly misleading because they elide ageing with old age or sickness. In fact we're all ageing from the moment we're born: you could say that birth causes age – ageing certainly isn't possible without it. As soon as you understand ageing as something that happens throughout the life cycle – taking place right now to us all, whatever our age – you begin to see it in a different perspective from the standard one in which we're young and then, hey presto, once we reach a certain threshold (25, 30, 40, 50 – take your pick), we cross over into 'ageing'.

That view, so culturally entrenched, is hard to shake off. It's certainly the case that most young people long to grow older – they associate ageing with the freedom to do things hitherto forbidden them. When can I stay up till ten? When am I allowed to go to a music festival on my own? I can't wait to turn 18 and buy alcohol legally. When you're young, ageing means freeing yourself from the tyranny of parents, making choices for yourself and gaining more control over your own life. Ageing, when you're a child, is viewed entirely as the medium through which your capabilities (to walk and talk, write and reason) develop and is toasted as the route to independence. It used to be your twenty-first but now it's your eighteenth, a birthday that shouts 'At last!'

But then, almost imperceptibly, this view of ageing begins to change: for most of us, probably in our twenties, anticipation and optimism come to be joined, sometimes replaced, by anxiety and even dread. The brief interlude of freedom without responsibilities ends, and the demands of adulthood, such as having to earn a living, hove into view. The prospect of life without six-week-long summer holidays is a truly shocking rite of passage. People now expect you to behave in ways that accord with their idea of an adult, with a seeming disregard for the fact that you may not feel like an adult, or even know what feeling like an adult might feel like. Growing older begins to seem more loss than gain, something to be resisted. By 25 one has the right to do pretty much everything one longed for earlier, and now the rest of life starts to roll out terrifyingly ahead. Alexa, 16, a London schoolgirl, told her aunt that she woke up in the middle of the night, worrying about how she'd know how to fill in a tax return when the time came.

Indeed many young people plump for 25 as the age that adulthood really begins. It isn't an entirely arbitrary age, for only at 25 are our frontal lobes fully developed, and the need for instant gratification modified by cognitive maturity, a greater capacity for empathy and a longer-term perspective. Twenty-five, as 24-year-old Becky put it with just a hint of alarm, is a quarter of a century old. It's when she plans to give up smoking, as if she'll become suddenly more susceptible to mortality on the morning of her twenty-fifth birthday. Or perhaps on that day it will have become finally undeniable.

How completely our attitudes change, within the space of a decade or two: from looking down on those younger (in the family, at school), to looking down on those older . . .

Ageing today

Ageing in the twenty-first century is a particularly confusing business. Today, 34 often looks like 24 a mere fifty years ago, and 44 like 34. But just because you look this way doesn't mean you are.

Traditionally, growing up meant leaving home: you had to separate from adults before you could become one. This, though, has become an increasingly extended process. We can salute the fact that some ideas about ageing have become less rigid, and that most of us feel less programmed to get a job, get married, buy a flat and have a child – all of these, in this order, at a prescribed age.

But tuition fees, high unemployment, the exorbitant cost of housing – all these mean that young people are financially reliant on their parents for far longer. 'Youth' used to be a short transitional phase between childhood and adulthood: today it can extend to your thirties. Parents are having to plough so much money into their kids that some expect a return for their investment. They also consider themselves entitled to a greater degree of involvement in their children's decisions – after all, they're paying for them – even though they may be ill-equipped to give advice about the new and unprecedented social realities that their kids are facing.

(In Ford cars there's now a feature which allows parents to control in advance the speed at which their children drive, along with programming insistent seat belt reminders and low-fuel warnings. It's like having your parent in the car along with you – a kind of Satnag. To the refrain 'get out of my life', adolescents will now be able to add 'get out of my car'.)

Increasing numbers of those in their twenties and thirties now fear growing up. The man-child holds on tightly to his video games and comics, and refuses to change. He equates being grown up with joylessness. But perhaps it's less about having a mortgage or a pension and more about learning to take responsibility for your spending; about being able to defer gratification instead of insisting 'I want it now'; about not saying the first thing that comes into your head and thinking about other people as well as yourself? Perhaps growing up is another way of saying that your perspective widens and lengthens. We need to rethink our ideas about what ageing means at every age, and not just old age.

Reversing age?

And yet even the perpetual adolescent, offered the chance to relive his teenage years, would probably refuse. All right, mutter those who decry the ageing process: perhaps there are some pleasures brought about by ageing, maybe being 15 wasn't the utopia we nostalgically re-imagine it to be. But wouldn't it be wonderful to go back to that earlier age with the knowledge accrued from this later one? To be younger but wiser – can there be a more common fantasy? Or a more preposterous one? It's like wanting your child to be born with the ability to walk, or able to recite Homer's *Odyssey* in Latin at the age of 3 – a petulant, infantile, if altogether understandable, desire to obliterate time.

All sorts of films have re-imagined the life cycle and rearranged the ages: from *Big* (1988), in which Tom Hanks plays a 12-year-old

The Curious Case of Benjamin Button: Rearranging the ages, this character is born with the appearance and maladies of an old man and ages in reverse.

boy transposed into the body of a 30-year-old man; to *18 Again!* (1988), where an 81-year-old man played by George Burns swaps bodies with his 18-year-old grandson; to *The Curious Case of Benjamin Button* (2008), based on the Scott Fitzgerald short story, in which Brad Pitt's character is born with the appearance and maladies of an old man and ages in reverse.

We can read in these popular-culture fantasies a generation wrestling with the meaning of age. They end either sadly or with the protagonist reverting to their real age – of course they do, because we age in concert with our peer group (to be singled out as the exception is a lonely experience), and at a particular historical period. We're a mulch of personal but also social and cultural memories. It's a completely different experience to grow older in the early twenty-first century, for instance, when being young is looked upon as a distinct, enviable and prolonged state, than it was in, say, the 1940s, before the arrival of teen clothing and culture, when adulthood was so admired and young people couldn't wait to cultivate all the appurtenances of adulthood – to look and sound like grown-ups.

There were all sorts of reasons for this cultural shift, including the development of the market. Before the 1960s you were either a child or an adult – there wasn't much in between – and this was reflected in the kinds of clothes and leisure opportunities available. But economic growth and the invention of the teenager gave birth to a whole new, age-segmented category of consumer. At the same time youthfulness came to be so prized that today, it sometimes seems, adults just want to look and sound like their kids.

But of course we can't go back. Human existence is temporal; as the Zen Buddhists put it, being cannot be apart from time. We live

Before the 1960s you were either a child or an adult – there wasn't much in between.

inside time: that of our own individual life but also of our generation, and the era into which we're born. Ageing is always not just a physiological but also a psychological, intellectual, social and cultural process – the idea that it's simply a case of swapping responsibilities for play does real injustice to the complexity and richness of the experience. Our bodies change but at the same time (unless we rigidly, compulsively, repeat old patterns) we mature; ageing is therefore less about the old and more about the new. Our brains, our minds, our relational capacities – given enough food, love, health and encouragement – all develop and grow. Indeed the capacity to play (especially among those in whom it was stunted in childhood) can effloresce with age. How can this be anything other than a cause for celebration?

If you want to play the decade-switching game, instead of imagining yourself younger but with your current level of knowledge and maturity, try playing it the other way round: what would my younger self feel about myself now? Except in those who nursed absurdly inflated expectations when they were young, most people trying this age-shift come up with the same 'if only': if only I had realized then that life would get better.

Proud to be older

Parents take delight in watching their children develop. Is it possible to take satisfaction from a similar process in oneself – from observing the way we weather life's difficulties, for instance? This isn't narcissism: it's self-help in the truest sense of the word. For most of us, growth and maturation are hard-won, and a source of satisfaction – we wouldn't want to forsake them. We enjoy our older self; we're grateful to have been allowed to develop. Ageing, whether at 10, 20, 30 or 40, is rewarding, or can be. By contrast, those who scare younger people with platitudes about schooldays being the best years of their life, or single out their student days as their happiest times, reveal more about their own lives and their sad inability to change than about ageing itself.

Of course different people are happiest at different times of their life, but what does it say about a person if they wag their fingers at young people and tell them reprovingly that they never had it so good? Or if they talk, however flippantly, about being 'the wrong side of 30'? And what stereotypical attitudes are exposed in a younger person who asks someone older how was it 'in your day'? Lucy, a 63-year-old teacher from Manchester, gently informed her son when he used this phrase that 'actually, today is my day, and so will tomorrow be.'

There is no template for 'ageing well'. It may be a cliché deployed to comfort the bereaved but nevertheless it's true: some people who die young pack more living into their short lifespan than others who survive to advanced old age. Similarly we each of us grow and mature in idiosyncratic ways: young people can be wise and old people idiots, and vice versa; most of us are by turns wise and idiotic – in the same week, the same day, sometimes the same hour. Life is constant flux, but age stereotypes arrest it, deadening us like pressed flowers. The idea, for example, that young people are indefatigable hedonists, forever in search of their next pleasure-fix, surgically attached to social media, utterly belies the fact that young people are more prone to wrestle with life's meaning and purpose than older and often more cynical adults. Frequently dismissed and mocked as youthful angst, in reality the questions they raise are ones that thoughtful, sensitive individuals return to throughout their lives.

Cultivating what's important

We can help the process if we think of ourselves like wine connoisseurs laying down bottles that will improve with age; similarly we can try to foster in ourselves qualities that deepen and enrich over the years. These qualities differ for each of us but for most people they include finding enduring sources of meaning – in work, or through relationships, interests or making a social contribution; getting to know themselves; making genuine contact with other people; and developing the capacity to love – whether people, ideas or experiences. These are essentially internal resources that can be cultivated and drawn upon throughout life. If we think about our entire lifespan, as I suggest in Chapter 7, scary though this is, it's easier to see what resources are necessary for the journey and begin to understand how to husband them.

All this sounds sobering, as though frivolity and fun drain away with the passing of time – no wonder people try to stuff them into their younger years. But the ability to laugh, like any other emotional facility, develops through use, and finding oneself convulsed with laughter, decades after childhood when it's so common, is sweet indeed.

Going forward into ageing

What would it be like to relish ageing? To continue, after the age of 25, to say 'I hope to grow older. I hope to grow old'? To genuinely look forward to ageing and not, at best, merely tolerate it? At this point, cynics will direct you to Voltaire's novella *Candide*, in which the tutor, Pangloss, regularly intones that 'all is for the best'. But although Voltaire was satirizing the follies of unbridled optimism, he didn't extol pessimism, concluding instead that 'we must cultivate our garden'. Pragmatic optimism like this is all that I am advocating here. It's much easier to adopt this outlook if we don't take a long lifespan for granted, but recognize instead that it isn't given to the majority of people in the world, especially the developing world: that to age is in fact to be blessed. The idea of age as a privilege seems radical in a culture where it's so often seen as a burden, but it's an invaluable reminder of how relatively recent, and limited, widespread longevity is.

Those who age best are those who travel lightest, who can jettison the prescriptive ideas they've cleaved to at one stage of their life when they find them ill-suited to another. A certain suppleness of spirit is needed. But the mantras of self-help, though they flow easily, invariably make things sound more effortless than they really are. Letting go of old narratives can be an extremely painful business: it involves mourning what never happened as well as what did, and admitting failure, wrong-headedness and poor decisions. Most unforgivably, it demands that we recognize that life unfurls beyond our control.

Freud made the crucial distinction between 'acting out' – the compulsive re-enactment of trauma – and 'working through', in which a person remembers traumatic events, losses or bereavements but reaches an accommodation with them, allowing them to change and so restoring vitality. Sometimes we need professional help to accomplish the task. But it's an enormously important aspect of the ageing process because it's the means through which we shed surplus baggage as we pass through life.

How different the life cycle looks if we substitute the word 'growth' for ageing. The word 'age' has become so contaminated by contempt and fear that it's tempting to dispense with it altogether. Better, though, to try to reclaim it, detoxify it and attach it to the whole life cycle, rather than just offloading the idea of ageing onto later life. For to age is to live and to live is to age, and being anti-age (as so many products proudly proclaim themselves) is tantamount to being anti-life. By embracing age we embrace the life process itself, with all its pain, joy and difficulty. If we can cultivate a respect for our own growth, and develop the ability to greet our ageing self with both pleasure and realism, and without the need to either idealize or deride its younger incarnation, then we're putting in place important capacities that will serve us our entire life.

The next chapter shows just how ageist modern life can be, so it might sound odd to say that never has thinking about the process of growing older been more exciting. A major grant-giving body calls itself the 'New Dynamics of Ageing' and, as the experience of ageing is increasingly being held up to public scrutiny and challenged, it's a good name – for the possibilities of a new dynamic of ageing are emerging both collectively and individually. The following pages give examples of people ageing creatively. This doesn't necessarily mean engaging in creative activity, but rather applying their imagination and adaptability to the business of ageing, and finding ways of living zestfully as they pass through the different stages of life, in spite of the disappointments and losses they meet along the way.

Ageing zestfully – not a bad motto.

2. Fear of Ageing

'There's nothing tragic about being 50. Not unless you're trying to be 25'

— Sunset Boulevard, 1950

In 2013 a 42-year-old American actress sued a website for revealing her age. 'If one is perceived to be "over the hill", i.e. approaching 40, it is nearly impossible for an up-and-coming actress . . . to get work', read her lawsuit, 'as she is thought to have less of an "upside".'

Two years earlier a Californian woman admitted that, to help her 8-year-old daughter – a beauty-pageant contestant – get rid of the 'wrinkles' that appeared on the girl's face when she smiled, she injected her with Botox. Said her daughter, 'I check every night for wrinkles; when I see some I want more injections. They used to hurt, but now I don't cry that much.' Ignominy rained down on her mother – it's so comforting to find someone we can all agree to hate. But she'd only pushed a cultural trend to its extreme. When is it acceptable to start Botoxing yourself or your children? Just-past-teens is now apparently a perfectly unremarkable age to start worrying about looking older.

The next few pages lay out how ageing is popularly represented. You'll notice that, whenever the subject is raised, both popular culture and political discussion immediately gravitate to old age, as though ageing were solely the business of our last decade or so of

Said an 8-year-old beauty pageant contestant, not much older than these ones, 'I check every night for wrinkles; when I see some I want more injections.'

life. This view is reflected in the representations of ageing that follow, even though they're a travesty of what ageing as a lifelong process really entails. They haven't been included to depress you, although, if you've passed the last few decades in another solar system, they may shock you. To experience the ageing process differently, we need to draw on an alternative model of getting older: one that recognizes that the process starts at birth, never stops and always has the potential to enrich our lives.

But we also have to learn to recognize and name the rampant gerontophobia – an irrational fear of old people and dread of ageing – that we've come to take for granted, in order to constantly challenge it.

Grey aliens

Those who denigrate old age have what seems to be the most powerful weapon of all at their disposal: demographics. By 2050, 20 per cent of the world's population will be 65 or over; Britain alone expects 50 per cent more people of this age by 2030, and a doubling of those over 85.

The West is certainly living through an unprecedented change in the age structure of the population, one which has inverted the population pyramid: for the first time – the result of falling birth rates at least as much as increased longevity – there are more people over 65 than under 16. By 2034, it's predicted that the 'old-age support ratio' (the number of people of working age to every person who's retired) will have fallen to 2.8, from 3.6 in 1971.

But these figures aren't just presented as a demographic fact; they're also used to fan fear. The language is apocalyptic: an 'agequake', a 'demographic timebomb' or even a 'grey tsunami' (take your pick of the catastrophe metaphors). We're no longer at risk of an invasion of triffids or Martians but of old people – invariably portrayed as a major social problem and a drain on resources, rather than as a resource themselves.

But, as the independent think tank Demos has pointed out, the whole debate about increasing longevity makes dubious alarmist assumptions about who's financially dependent on whom. In reality, increasing numbers of us of 'working age' today are unemployed, while growing numbers continue to work beyond state-pension age, so you can no longer neatly correlate age with economic activity.

And when it comes to care and support, ageist assumptions are even less accurate. Older people provide as much care as they receive: those aged 75 or over spend more time looking after someone, usually a partner, than young people – not to mention the informal but essential childcare being provided by so many grandparents. Is this being 'economically inactive'?

Of course an ageing population throws up genuine dilemmas, particularly for women, who most often end up responsible for looking after older family members. It also undoubtedly creates extra costs and new needs, although the economist Phil Mullan, in his book *The Imaginary Time Bomb*, systematically dismantles the argument that ageing represents an unsupportable burden for industrialized societies. The debate about the financial costs of old people, he suggests, has been deliberately exaggerated, partly to shift responsibility for their financial support away from the state and onto private providers and older individuals themselves.

The 'burden' model of ageing isn't new: Anthony Trollope satirized it in 1881 in his dystopian novel *The Fixed Period*. In the ex-British colony of Britannula in 1980, the President and Chamber have come up with a novel solution to the problem of a world burdened with 'those who remain to live a useless and painful life' – i.e. the aged. The day its citizens reach 67 (interestingly, Trollope's own age when the book was published) the 'fixed period' of life requires them to submit to euthanasia. But when the first (and, unfortunately, vigorous) candidate nears the appointed hour, his urge to stay alive and his family and neighbours' revulsion towards the policy create a major social crisis, one only ended by the intervention of the English.

What makes the burden model all the more bizarre is that it's mostly put about by those very people who themselves are going to constitute this large cohort of the elderly. These commentators – the majority young adults or middle-aged – are peddling the frightening prospect of an invasion of old people draining public finances, seemingly oblivious of the fact that they're describing themselves!

But 'them' never becomes 'us'; it's as if they've dealt with their own fears of ageing by displacing them onto the population at large. Or by assuming that the current cohort of old people will somehow obligingly stay on and continue to occupy the role in perpetuity, so that those who are now 30 to 50 will never have to take their place: today's oldies will remain tomorrow's oldies. And thus they condemn themselves to a kind of prolonged infantilism. What they don't realize is that they're banking disgust that they'll have to draw on themselves – *ourselves*.

Indeed gerontologists, who study the process of growing old, have puzzled over this unique feature of ageism: that it's prejudice against one's future self. In this it differs from other kinds of prejudice and discrimination like sexism and racism. It's fuelled, as we'll see, by a refusal to admit that we too will age – by a profound dis-identification with old people. Or indeed that we are all, all the time, already ageing.

The helpless old

To detoxify ageing, to make it possible for us to think of ourselves as ageing, we need to throw off the caricatures of old people. Older people, for example, are almost invariably described as lonely, and there are some brilliant fictional portrayals of lonely old people. Clare Temple in Norah Hoult's remarkable 1944 novel, *There Were No Windows*, is a woman aware of her creeping dementia: 'When one hasn't any more friends, then one makes friends with one's chairs and tables. I say, "Well, at least *you've* stayed with me all these years."' And then there's Elizabeth Taylor's marvellously astute novel *Mrs Palfry at the Claremont* (1971): 'She knew that, as she got older, she looked at her watch more often, and that it was always earlier than she had thought it would be. When she was young, it had always been later.'

It's good that fiction explores this important aspect of human experience. And who can complain about campaigns launched by well-meaning charities to alleviate loneliness among 'the elderly' at Christmas? Yet when older people in all their diversity are so absent

Who can complain about campaigns launched by well-meaning charities to alleviate loneliness among 'the elderly' at Christmas? Yet such campaigns inadvertently encourage us to see them almost exclusively through the prism of vulnerability.

from popular culture, such campaigns inadvertently encourage us to see them almost exclusively through the prism of vulnerability. Nearly 1 in 5 old people may be lonely, but more than 4 in 5 presumably aren't. Of course we shouldn't wave away concerns about loneliness in old age on this account, but focusing on it so relentlessly makes it come to be seen as an inevitable, essential attribute of old age, understandably scaring those who are younger.

If it is true that not all old people who live alone are lonely, it's also true that many young people are. Indeed in an era where young people are assumed to be permanently texting and clubbing, perhaps there's more stigma attached to being lonely and young than old. But you're not going to be seeing a campaign about this any time soon . . .

Frailty is another persistent image of old age. In December 2012 a 90-year-old woman had to be evacuated from her flooded home in Somerset. Most of the newspaper and television reports framed this in an 'old vulnerable victim' way. In fact she'd retreated to the first floor of her farmhouse, determined to sit out the floods, until a power cut meant that she had no heat and couldn't make herself a cup of tea. This wasn't victimhood but resilience, self-reliance and stoicism.

Yet popular culture can't seem to find a language to represent this aspect of age. Shakespeare's King Lear, raging against the waning of his powers, has metamorphosed, in modern society, into Norma Desmond (Gloria Swanson), the faded movie star in Billy Wilder's film *Sunset Boulevard*, raging against Hollywood and the talkies: all is loss, shrinkage.

Gloria Swanson in *Sunset Boulevard*: Norma Desmond, the faded movie star, rages against Hollywood and the talkies.

Contemptible bodies

Artists, too, find it hard to portray the aged body realistically and at the same time lovingly and respectfully. Many Renaissance and baroque artists depicted old age as a time of 'hideous ruin', but there was no sadism or contempt in Rembrandt's portraits of age, only dignity, a deep empathy still moving centuries later. Albrecht Dürer's 1514 charcoal sketch of his 63-year-old mother showed her face gaunt and wrinkled, that of a woman who'd given birth eighteen times, and yet with a kind of grandeur about her.

Lucian Freud painted his own ageing body beautifully – it remained strong and muscular under his gaze. But look at his unflinching portraits of the faces of older friends, family and models: unsentimental, yes, but also dispassionate – an almost clinical examination of decay.

In the hands of lesser artists this becomes what sociologist Mike Featherstone has called 'a pornography of old age', a luxuriating in disgust. You find the same quality in some writers, especially female, who've dealt with their own discomfort about ageing by turning their humorous eye onto their own bodily changes. The doyenne of this deprecated female body was Nora Ephron, in *I Feel Bad About My Neck*:

> Oh the necks. There are chicken necks. There are turkey-gobbler necks. There are elephant necks. There are necks with wattles and necks with creases that are on the verge of becoming wattles. There are scrawny necks and fat necks, loose necks, crêpey necks, banded necks, wrinkled necks,

Albrecht Dürer's sketch of his 63-year-old mother showed her face gaunt and wrinkled, yet with a kind of grandeur about her.

stringy necks, flabby necks, mottled necks . . . You have to
cut open a redwood tree to see how old it is, but you wouldn't
have to if it had a neck.

In this gallery of the grotesque, the reader has only different varieties
of animal with which to identify. Or a tree.

Age is all

One problem with growing old in our culture is that everything
comes to be seen through the prism of age. American psychologist Elissa Melamed, in her wonderful book *Mirror, Mirror: The
Terror of Not Being Young*, published thirty years ago, tells the story
of a 70-year-old woman who visited her doctor to complain about
her painful right knee: 'You're 70 years old, what do you expect?' he
asked. 'But my left knee is 70 too,' she retorted, 'and it's fine.' Older
people are rarely referred for psychotherapy (and not just because of
Freud's view, rebuffed down the years, that their mental processes
aren't elastic enough to make them suitable), because depression is
seen as just another inevitable aspect of old age.

The icons of old age are all about infirmity – bath chairs, stairlifts
and Zimmer frames. The road sign for elderly people is a hunched
woman and a man clutching a cane (an image that Age UK five years
ago complained was outdated). Now we may want to de-stigmatize
dependency, as I suggest in Chapter 7, but first we need to topple
it from its prime position as emblem of age, along with slippers,
dentures and hearing aids. Not because there's anything wrong with

these things (on the contrary, let's hear it for dentures and hearing aids!), but because they're used to generalize old people, and identify them not with abilities but disabilities.

Cinema is particularly at fault. If you're old in movies you're almost certainly miserly, deaf or depressed (this latter hardly surprising, given the poverty of the lines you have to utter). Or a witch, crone or curmudgeon. You can either be demonized or patronized – take your pick.

But perhaps the most pernicious stereotype of old age – and the competition is keen – is that it's a 'second childhood'. In the words of anthropologists Jenny Hockey and Allison James, 'elderly people have been transformed into metaphoric children.'

Jaques's 'seven ages' speech in Shakespeare's *As You Like It* is partly to blame:

> Last scene of all,
> That ends this strange eventful history,
> Is second childishness and mere oblivion,
> Sans teeth, sans eyes, sans taste, sans everything.

If we want to detoxify ageing for ourselves, let's start here. The idea that senescence is the mirror image of childhood, with each of the capacities then acquired now relinquished – a kind of 'last in, first out' – is a particularly nasty example of the narrative of decline, obliterating a person's entire life experience in the process.

There's one kind of person, though, who, no matter their age, escapes this fate. They'll never be consigned to the catch-all category of 'pensioner', but, alas, you can't elect to join them: they're the older celebrity. Fame seems to trump age as a defining label. Whether you're the Queen or Paul McCartney, David Hockney or Oprah Winfrey, Hillary Clinton or Maya Angelou, your celebrity will almost certainly expose you to critical media scrutiny, especially if you're a woman, but in return you won't be seen as old or be referred to as an old person: this is what cultural power buys you.

Denying Age

Since we last met them, Gina's parents have been busy. Her mother, Sara, rushes from her dermal-filler injections to her personal trainer. Gina's father, Clive, meanwhile, has set up a company organizing 'grey gap years', and has started to take the human-growth hormone, prescribed by an American doctor friend of his, that promises to reverse the signs of ageing. Baby boomers both, at 56 and 62 respectively, they're convinced that they and their peers have redefined ageing, and can think, supplement and exercise old age away. Or at least postpone it. Unflagging Sara and Clive are examples of the 'third age'.

The term originated in France in the 1970s but was popularized in Britain by Peter Laslett in 1989, who placed it between the second age of adulthood and the fourth age of dependency and ill-health. Once the children had grown up and the most intensive demands of paid work were over, he argued, healthy, active and educated people needed to put their abilities to good use, and not consign themselves to a life of nothing but hobbies.

The fourth age

In many respects Laslett was prescient, helping develop the University of the Third Age, for instance. But there's a terrible flaw here. The idea of 'the third age' – a period of adventure and personal growth for the healthy and moneyed – requires the existence of a later 'fourth age', into which can be corralled all those luckless older souls, or poor, unhealthy middle-aged ones, who aren't in any position to swap the ski lift for the stairlift. In order for our fifties, sixties, seventies and early eighties to be reconceived as 'not old', those in their late eighties and early nineties (along with those who've aged 'badly') have to agree to be 'only old'.

Indeed, when it came to the very old, Laslett's book, *A Fresh Map of Life*, wasn't quite so fresh. If the third age was the age of fulfilment, the fourth was nothing other than the age of decline – or 'dependence and decrepitude', as he so charmingly styled it – for the only role that Laslett saw for fourth-agers was a complete withdrawal from life. Perhaps he was a pioneer in this regard, too, for his attitude to the 'old old' is now widespread, and the fourth age has come to be seen as a kind of antechamber of death, its entrance boarded up by third-agers determined to escape its embrace.

Sara, as she swallows her glucosamine and does her daily Sudoku to keep her joints and mind supple, has signed up enthusiastically to the concept of 'successful ageing'. She and her friends believe this is achieved through willpower and choice – for to become one of the 'new aged' the price you pay isn't just the cost of gym membership: you need to be constantly vigilant, eternally self-monitoring. (And, if you're a woman, remember especially not to 'let yourself go' – as if your self were entirely a property of your youth and could go AWOL.)

It doesn't take long to work out how dangerous this way of thinking is. We've created a new stereotype – that of the mobile, healthy and affluent 'new old', which at the same time demonizes the immobile, sick and poor 'old old'. It's as if old age these days only befalls those too powerless, poor or stupid to do something about it. Those who shamefully surrender to the ageing process surely deserve what they get – 'unsuccessful ageing', since third-agers like Sara and Clive have convinced themselves that, with enough discipline and self-control, the body can always be transcended. But it can't.

Perhaps this is why Michael Haneke's award-winning film *Amour* so stunned audiences: it showed how the lives of a sophisticated, educated and affluent bourgeois couple could be suddenly devastated by a stroke – hers. Against this, no amount of glucosamine and Sudoku would have been remotely effective.

For the truth is that we all have to go into that good night eventually, gently or otherwise – to deny this is nothing more than magic thinking. Sure, moisturize all you want, exercise away – of course staying mobile is good and looking after yourself important. But those anti-ageing nostrums and elixirs that promise to freeze the ageing process? Why, they're simply re-stigmatizing ageing all over again, even as they pretend to de-stigmatize it. And the magazine articles that tell you 'How To Look Fabulous At Fifty', or extol the arrival of the 'yummy granny'? They encourage you to deal with the prejudice against old people not by challenging it but by trying not to look old.

They're just gerontophobia in its latest incarnation. We're (almost) all Dorian Grays now, demanding that the fourth-agers do

our ageing for us: that they agree to be old so that the rest of us don't
have to.

Sara and Clive aren't stupid. Deep in their fish-oil-supplemented
marrow they know that, like some black people in the pre-civil-rights
period who tried to 'pass' as white, they're trying to 'pass' as younger.
But Clive reasons that he's just facing up to the reality identified by
Steve Martin in the film *Bowfinger*: 'Employers can smell 50'.

Sara and Clive also know that none of these age-resisting strategies are available to Dolores, their 63-year-old Spanish cleaner, who
brought up four children single-handed and looks old enough to be
their grandmother; the nearest she gets to doing step aerobics is
hoovering their stairs.

The profits of fear

Sara may be hooked on Estée Lauder's 'Advanced Night Repair', but
she doesn't like the implication that ageing entails a breakage of
some kind. Nor does she warm to those creams that call themselves
'mature-skin corrector', as if ageing were nature's mistake. She uses
a lotion called 'Time Delay', though of course she knows that it can't.
Sara realizes that she's never seen a product or service labelled 'pro-
age', nor does she even understand what it would mean to be pro-age.

This is hardly surprising since the fears of ageing baby boomers
have proved enormously lucrative – the anti-ageing market is predicted
to reach over $290 billion (£180 billion) globally by 2015. The third age
is now all about consumption – products, procedures and leisure activities. Anyone for anti-ageing chocolate? Or a 'nutraceutical' capsule
'scientifically developed to make you look and feel younger'?

Even though Gina has only just reached 30, her own self-surveillance has already begun. Indeed skin creams target not only those wrinkles already visible but also those 'programmed: waiting to appear in the future.' Unwrinkled, in this formulation, doesn't exist: the best you can be is pre-wrinkled. Supposedly rejuvenating lotions are modelled by 30-year-old women, even though we all know that they didn't have any wrinkles for the lotion to erase in the first place.

But there's another reason why young women of Gina's age advertise these products: because this is who the advertiser's target audience is – anxious 30-year-olds. A 2002 survey found that fear of ageing was no longer confined to 35- to 49-year-olds but had spread even to 20-year-olds.

The beauty industry, in particular, has discovered how many more products it can sell if it segments the market, with different versions targeted at women in their twenties, thirties, forties and fifties (presumably after this you're on your own). Anxieties about ageing now set in so early that Carrie, who is 25, reports that almost all of her friends except her have already had Botox. Maggie Kuhn, the leader of the Gray Panthers, said to me in 1978 that the surest sign of change would be when 'you look your age' became a compliment. That day seems further away than ever.

Them and Us

But what if Aubrey de Grey, author of *Ending Aging*, is right when he talks of rejuvenation breakthroughs that could reverse human ageing in our lifetime – would any of us pass up the opportunity? Is there really anything wrong with seeing yourself as an ageless 'amortal', or a 'rejuvenile', if it liberates you from the prison of ageing?

Well, yes, if such hubris also entails contempt for old people, and is another version of age shame. It also may come back to bite you if, in spite of your best efforts, your body starts to 'betray' your years. It's all very well intoning 'use it or lose it', but this doesn't allow for the possibility that you may still lose it despite using it.

In any case, ageing is not just a 'state of mind', despite the slogan – it's one of the most important dimensions of life. 'You are not only as old as you feel,' the sociologist Molly Andrews argued in her brilliant essay 'The seductiveness of agelessness', 'you are also as old as you are.' The concept of agelessness, she suggests, erases our experience, strips us of our history and leaves us with nothing but mimicry of our youth.

Who can blame Sara and Clive if, in such a gerontophobic culture, they strive to distance themselves from old people now holed up safely in the category of 'Them'. Since old age is so stigmatized, most of us do everything we can to dis-identify with it. Think of it: in our culture, 'to feel your age' is a synonym for feeling bad and lacking vitality. Just imagine if it connoted wisdom and experience.

Sara and Clive are part of the 'exceptionalist' tendency: other people, they concede, may age, but they won't. This means, as sociologist Sarah Matthews has pointed out, that you have one definition for other ageing people, and one for yourself. How isolating! It prevents you from making common cause with other older people. So a 61-year-old woman, responding to a Mass Observation survey, observed that 'If I go into a room and all around me I see grey heads I tend to assume that I'm in a gathering of the elderly – for one awful moment I stereotype a lot, forgetting, honestly, that I am among their number.' This is prejudice not towards one's future self, but towards one's present.

The impact of ageism

The effects of the prejudices lined up here are even more powerful than we consciously realize. In their study comparing the memory of young and old Chinese and Americans, social psychologist Ellen Langer and epidemiologist Becca Levy found that the older Chinese, exposed to less ageism than their American counterparts, performed memory tests more like younger Chinese. Among the Americans, on the other hand, there were significant differences between the old and young. So the beliefs that we imbibe about our waning powers may turn out be self-fulfilling, because our culture teaches us how to be old.

In fact, Levy has gone so far as to claim that these stereotypes can actually affect our survival. Her 2002 study concluded that older people with a more positive perception of ageing lived seven-and-a-half years longer than those with a more negative one.

On the other hand, by believing that 'middle age' is infinitely extendible, we cheat ourselves of the possibility of a good old age. A 1996 American survey asked 50-year-olds when old age began: the average age they plumped for was 79.5 years – this is when the average life expectancy of Americans was 76.1. So they really did hope they died before they got old.

The third way

This is a book about how to age and not about how not to, but we've started here because the first stage in age-acceptance is to identify and name those social currents that militate against it, that work to prevent us from wanting anything to do with the ageing process. By scrutinizing and then refusing the dominant myths about ageing we can begin to understand that our own ageing experience will be particular to us: you don't have to trade in your personal subjectivity for a free bus pass. We'll also start to appreciate that *joie de vivre* can intensify through age, and that you can be a more joyful person at 36 than at 26.

There's another approach to ageing, but it requires a major gestalt switch: each time we see an older person, we need to imagine them as our future self, and, rather than recoil from their wrinkles or infirmities, applaud their resilience. We need to re-humanize older people, to attribute to them the same rich internal world, set of passions and network of complex human relationships that we assume exist in younger people and in ourselves.

Prejudice leads to abuse: those caring for old people, whether relatives or in residential care, are more likely to treat them carelessly or abusively after years of exposure to stereotypes that effectively dehumanize them. If we accepted that we, too, will one day become old, we'd be clamouring for generous pay for those who might have to help look after us.

The rewards of seeing ageing in this way are enormous. In another study, Levy and her colleagues filmed older people before and after watching a computer game that emitted subliminal positive or negative messages about old age and the ageing process. Those who'd received the positive messages walked faster, and with a greater spring in their step.

No one is pretending that shifting our thinking is easy, or can be done in isolation. But, happily, the constant vigilance that you need to resist the denigration and denial of ageing is no greater – and is probably less – than the vigilance you need to ensure that you don't betray the slightest signs of ageing. At some point or other, age-resistance becomes frankly futile – you'll either die or start to look old – but the energy you use to accept the fact of ageing but refuse its stereotypes will serve you well for the rest of your life. If there ever was an insurance policy that could help enrich the process of getting older, it's this refusal to pathologize age, this spirited age-acceptance – of *living* time rather than trying to stop it.

Older can be happier

Although it's easy to find horror stories about old people's lives and living conditions, for most of us the reality is different. In fact reams of research show that people become happier as they age, whether through developing new emotional strategies or simply through a change in priorities (less striving for outward achievements, more savouring of relationships). But we mis-predict that we'll become less happy as we age.

The poet Sharon Olds put it beautifully in 'The Older', where she describes how lovable and 'almost beautiful' she finds her ageing body, which her younger self would have found repugnant.

Pete Townshend of The Who famously sang 'Hope I die before I get old'. On his sixtieth birthday he declared that he was much happier than when he'd written those words.

3. Embracing Age

When Howard and Gisele Miller, both in their seventies, emerged from the Washington DC subway they hit a problem. There was no way that they could walk to their daughter and son-in-law's house for dinner in the snowstorm that was then raging. They needed a cab, but no cabs were stopping in the rush hour. They tried calling the house – this was before the advent of the mobile – but no one was home yet. As their fingers started to go numb Howard noticed a pizza restaurant across the street. He and Giselle went in and ordered a large pizza for home delivery. When the sales assistant asked for the delivery address, Howard gave it and added, 'Oh, there's one more thing.' 'What's that?' asked the assistant. 'We want you to deliver us with it.' And so they arrived, along with a giant pizza, for dinner that night.

The Millers' solution exhibited a resourcefulness that would be admirable at any age, but their son-in-law, Gene Cohen, an American gerontologist, tells the story to illustrate the kind of agile creativity that the ageing mind is capable of. It's the total opposite of the calcified thinking usually attributed to older people. For the narrative of decline would have us believe that, upon receipt of the state pension – if not considerably earlier – our vital juices desiccate and our life force atrophies: we're spent. Time, it suggests, is a thief: the night before our sixtieth birthday it creeps in and cleans out our mind and heart, replacing them with an infusion of Old Age. The third-agers, understandably, find such an attitude so unbearable that they simply reverse it: nothing changes with age – it's just a number.

Loss and gain

A false opposition like this denies the fact that our lives, from their very beginning, are a constant interplay between continuity and transformation. As Molly Andrews put it,

> Throughout the lifecycle, change and continuity weave an intricate web. As we meet the new challenges, both physical and psychological, with which our lives confront us, so then we are changed, even as we remain the same. Old age is no different from the other stages of life in this regard. The changes are many and real; to deny them, as some do in an attempt to counter ageism, is folly.

One of the greatest challenges of ageing, perhaps, is to recognize what endures and what changes. To those who neither deny ageing, nor close down upon life prematurely, this happens instinctively. If ageing is embraced, then we inevitably recognize that some things are no longer possible and we mourn them. So, for example, an older woman might find her creeping invisibility hard to bear, especially if she's invested a lot in her appearance.

On the other hand she may actually find it a relief: now she's freer to do what she wants without anxieties about her appearance or the need for approval getting in the way. (Of course there's a third possibility: she may never stop delighting in dressing and decorating herself, for her own pleasure and self-expression, no matter the date on her birth certificate.)

Although it might seem paradoxical, mourning is an essential part of ageing with gusto, because it helps you say goodbye to some features of life, freeing you to welcome in new ones. But this isn't a process confined to old age. A child may articulate it through tears rather than words, but when they start school they may mourn the loss of the unstructured time they've enjoyed up till then. Similarly, finishing school is generally celebrated as a wonderful liberation, making it shameful to admit to some sadness about the losses that accompany it: no more ready-made structure, or the (sometimes) consoling presence of parents. We may rebel against school and parents, but not having them there to rebel against is another matter altogether. Being able to tolerate some sadness and grief about necessary losses is a vital human resource to help us age – at any age.

Still me, after all these years

Unless we suffer from totally debilitating Alzheimer's (the magnet of all our anxieties about ageing these days), time doesn't steal a person's essence. We never become Them, but remain ourselves, only older. The journalist Peregrine Worsthorne admitted that

It is difficult for me to write about old age because I do not feel old. I simply feel myself. Perhaps I am abnormally, monstrously egocentric in this respect, since I also have to admit that I cannot remember ever having felt young or middle-aged. I can remember the kind of hopes, worries and fears I felt at different periods of my life, but it was the same me having those old worries, hopes and fears. And it is the unbroken continuity of my self-consciousness that makes the circumstantial changes seem relatively insignificant.

What would it be like to 'feel old'? Nobody seems to have ever defined it; it's more often used in the negative – 'I don't feel old' – than in the positive. When people say they feel old they emit a vague sense of weariness, which is often actually depression and not an intrinsic part of ageing at all. Or they're referring to the way they're treated by others, like employers. And when they say that they don't feel old, they're referring to the stereotypes of age that they themselves may have held. The *Guardian* newspaper ran a feature in 2013 in which it asked various of its writers how old they felt. Of the six they canvassed, only one admitted to feeling their age; most of the others felt younger. But when a 70-year-old says that she feels 18, does this mean she feels like she did at 18, or how she thinks 18 feels? What does 18 feel like? And how does she imagine 70 feels?

The French writer André Gide, when he was 60, wrote that 'I have to make a great effort to convince myself that I am at present as old as those who seemed to me so ancient when I was young.' It's understandable, of course, that to a young person 60 seems old, but then so does 30. Or 21. Or even, when you are 4 years old, 5. Which of us hasn't known – or been – the 3-year-old who thinks that life will be utterly transformed on the morning of their fourth birthday? We've learnt to assume that age will bring radical discontinuities to our life, whether at 4 or 40. But it doesn't. Perhaps this is one of the truths about ageing that we find hardest to learn.

Most older people recognize in themselves the interplay between continuity and change identified by Andrews. Lucy, 63, says, 'If my younger self were to see me today, she'd recognize me – there's so much we have in common. At the same time she'd feel enormous relief to see how much happier I've become – I often wish I could tell her.'

Stella, 70, has been married to 76-year-old Paul for 40 years. 'When our children ask us how we can bear being with the same person for so long we say we haven't – we've both changed so much. But Paul still has the same 'Paulishness', his mischievous sparkle, that he had when I first met him. There's an old school photo of him at 13 and he had it then too.' In this respect we never need to lose our earlier selves, only add to them. These kinds of positive ideas about ageing aren't the preserve of older people: they can be developed at any stage of life. Similarly embracing age doesn't mean embracing old age, but accepting the very process of change that occurs as we move through life – it's as relevant when you move from 28 to 29 as when you pass from 58 to 59.

Still vital, after all these years

Perhaps the greatest calumny committed against old people – and the one that most frightens the not-yet-old – is the belief that ageing causes us to leech vitality. Let's not get too Pollyanna about this: most people find their energy levels changing as they age and have to learn to pace themselves (that's what siestas were invented for). Even 30-year-olds can be heard complaining that their stamina is receding along with their hairline, while all-night benders begin to exact increasingly large servings of revenge, usually in one's mid-twenties. But physical and mental vitality, though they may be related, especially if you're fighting pain, are not the same thing. The idea that one's appetite for life automatically abates with the passing of the years is simply wrong.

Cicero clocked this. People, said the Roman orator in *De Senectute*, his treatise on old age, 'who have no resources in themselves for securing a good and happy life find every age burdensome.' Only fools, he believed, imputed their own frailties to old age. Although some say he idealized old age, and his own was nothing like the one he wrote about, nevertheless he no more missed the bodily strength he had as a young man, he declared, than he missed the strength of a bull or elephant: 'The great affairs of life are not performed by physical strength, or activity, or nimbleness of body, but by deliberation, character, expression of opinion. Of these old age is not only not deprived but, as a rule, has them in a greater degree.'

One can be alive or dead at any age. In Hal Ashby's glorious 1971 black comedy, *Harold and Maude*, a lugubrious, depressed 19-year-old boy falls in love with a 79-year-old effervescent woman he meets at the funerals they frequent as a hobby. Infusing him with her vitality, she brings him to life.

Vitality can't be timetabled. Brecht's short story 'The Unseemly Old Lady' recounts the tale of a 72-year-old woman who had been a devoted mother and wife. But after her husband dies she 'permits herself certain liberties'. Flouting convention, she invites the priest to

Harold and Maude: A depressed 19-year-old boy falls in love with a 79-year-old effervescent woman he meets at the funerals they frequent as a hobby.

the cinema, gossips, and drinks at the cobblers. In her last two years 'she consumed the bread of life to the last crumb.' She represents one answer to those who say 'I should have . . .', who mark out the past with regrets instead of seeing what remains possible.

Perhaps the most delicious account of how growing older can mean growing more engaged was written by Florida Scott-Maxwell. This American-born playwright and suffragette, who later lived in Scotland and London, began a new career at the age of 40 when she started training as an analytical psychologist under Carl Jung. Scott-Maxwell lived until she was 96, and in *The Measure of My Days*, her marvellous book on ageing, published in 1968 when she was 85, she wrote:

> Age puzzles me. I thought it was a quiet time. My seventies were interesting and fairly serene, but my eighties are passionate. I grow more intense as I age. To my own surprise, I burst out with hot conviction. Only a few years ago, I enjoyed my tranquillity; now I am so disturbed by the outer world and by human quality in general that I want to put things right, as though I still owed a debt to life. I must calm down. I am far too frail to indulge in moral fervour.

A succession of psychoanalysts have made a similar observation – that passions needn't diminish over time. The first to think seriously about ageing was Erik Erikson, who argued that we pass through eight psychosocial stages through life. Erikson's stages look a little programmatic today, when our lives aren't quite so rigidly age-patterned, yet what's striking still about his interviews with older people is how, even if they were fairly inactive, they savoured their 'sensory attachment to life'. More recently the French psychotherapist Marie de Hennezel found exactly the same quality in the many older people that she interviewed: an 'ardent old age', consisting of curiosity, a capacity for joy and wonderment, the ability to learn and think, and sensuality. All of these, she believes, can withstand and survive even severe physical curtailment. In Hebrew, one word, *guil*, means both age and joy.

Of course all this uplift can be wearying. We shouldn't deprive ourselves of a little misanthropy, if we so choose, and complaining about the state of the world and our bodies surely ranks as one of the pleasures of life. But the caricature of the elderly as 'grumpy old men and women' doesn't discriminate between a bit of healthy moaning and the rage felt by many older people at the way our culture marginalizes, impoverishes and dismisses them.

The acrobatic brain

It's never too late to revitalize oneself, although you would be forgiven for not realizing this in our milestone society, so in love with precocity. Childcare manuals often encourage the idea that there's a 'correct age' to acquire certain skills – ageism of another kind, despite all the evidence demonstrating huge differences in when people develop. We grow up hearing about the importance of early learning, when the brain is supposedly at its most malleable, as though mental sclerosis inevitably sets in with the passage of time.

But recent research disproves this. As I pointed out earlier, there's evidence that the brain in midlife – roughly 35 to 65 and even beyond – remains plastic. According to George Bártzokis, a neurologist at the

University of California, Los Angeles, 'In midlife, you're beginning to maximize the ability to use the entirety of the information in your brain on an everyday, ongoing, second-to-second basis . . . you're able to use it better in everyday life.'

A long-term study from the University of California, tracking a group of women for almost forty years, came up with an even more startling finding. The women scored highest in their inductive reasoning between their early forties and sixties, while their ability to coolly evaluate contradictory ideas didn't peak until their fifties or sixties. Another longitudinal study confirmed that this was true for both men and women. As Barbara Strauch, author of *The Secret Life of the Grown-up Brain*, observes, for years most research into ageing was conducted in nursing homes, where bodies and brains are rarely stimulated, and this shaped beliefs about what it means to get old.

More recent research shows the value of experience and tacit knowledge. 'Verbatim memory' (listing things word-for-word, unit-by-unit) may decline with age but 'gist memory' (assembling and grouping concepts into categories) improves as we get older, when the hemispheres of the brain cooperate better.

What's more, just as individuals differ more and not less as they age, so too, it seems, do their brains. Research at the University of Cambridge challenges the idea of cognitive ageing as a monolithic process of universal, inexorable, progressive decline. In reality, cognitive functions remain stable across the adult lifespan in most of us to a great extent.

Like a muscle, the brain can continue to develop, especially when stimulated by physical exercise. So confining old people to a sedentary, immobile life – whether at home or in a home – is an ideal way to hasten their decline; unless you're totally paralysed, some form of movement is always possible.

Creative ageing

Creativity, like vitality, is unrelated to age. Darwin was 50 when *On the Origin of Species* appeared and Kant, 57 when *Critique of Pure Reason* was published. All of Defoe's novels were written when he was over 60. Goya was 66 when he began to paint *The Disasters of War*. (When he was 80 he drew an ancient man with a Father Christmas-style voluminous beard, bent over two sticks, with the inscription '*Aun aprendo*' – I'm still learning.) Verdi composed *Otello* at 72 and *Falstaff* at 76; Sophocles wrote *Oedipus Rex* at 68 and *Oedipus at Colonus* at 89. Picasso continued to paint until his death at 92.

In a famous paper, 'Death and the midlife crisis', first published in 1965, Elliot Jacques argued that between the ages of 35 and 65 the work of creative artists changes, from a 'hot' and intense creativity to a more 'sculpted' one. This, he believed, showed that they'd worked through some of the emotional conflicts that had raged in their earlier life and were coming to accept the inevitability of death.

There's a danger here, though, of replacing one stereotype with another: no longer wizened old crones or grumpy men, older people are now repositories of wisdom, the apotheosis of serenity. Yet many of us simply don't have a serenity gene, and if you aren't remotely serene in your twenties, there's no reason why you should suddenly

Goya was 80 when he drew this with the inscription '*Aun aprendo*' – I'm still learning.

metamorphose into some imperturbable guru just because you've turned 30 – or 60. This is to return to the child's fantasy of ageing, that an additional year or two will utterly transform you.

The critic Edward Said challenged the idea of late work as necessarily serene, exuding a sense of harmony and resolution. 'What if,' he asked, 'age and ill-health don't produce the serenity of "ripeness is all"?' When he examined the late work of Bach, Beethoven and Ibsen, Said found instead intransigence, difficulty and unresolved contradictions. Perhaps these are just an inevitable part of being fully alive.

Most of us aren't Bach or Beethoven, Ibsen or Picasso, of course, but 'Above Ground', a study by Columbia University of ageing artists in New York and their robust networks, suggested that we can learn a lot about dynamic ways of ageing from older creative artists. Interviewing 213 of them of them between the ages of 62 and 97 (no third-/fourth-age divide here), the study found they had a number of things in common: they went to their studio every day, even if it took them an hour and a half to walk two blocks; they communicated with other artists at least weekly, if not daily; some had changed medium into one that was less physically demanding. The majority agreed on a couple of other things. One was that they'd never retire – it would be tantamount to retiring from life. Another was that they were highly satisfied with their lives. This suggests that physical activity, work or an absorbing interest of some kind, as well as consciously maintaining social networks, both enrich the ageing process.

If we can't all be Goya, still, with a modicum of health (mental and physical) and money, we can replenish our lives and reinvent ourselves. After a high-flying career in television, Laura became a yoga teacher at 46, and an art student at 55:

I was looking for the next stage in my life, something more spiritual, and I discovered yoga. It fascinated me but it's quite precise, so I then wanted to make something with my hands that was freer. I had my first career for thirty years, and I think I'll probably keep up these two for another thirty. I don't regret that I didn't find them earlier because I loved what I did before: I wouldn't want to be doing it now but I loved it then and love what I'm doing now.'

Indeed growing older can make people more creative, and not less. Tim Dee is an accomplished radio producer, but it wasn't until he was 48 that he started writing creative non-fiction. *The Running Sky*, his glorious book about bird-watching, is really about the pleasures of looking and feeling. What took him so long to start writing? The over-critical voice developed in studying English at university, he says: time helped him find a voice of his own.

Jennie, 51, had always wanted to become an interpreter, but never had the confidence, so she took a succession of administrative jobs instead. Three years ago, when the last of her children left home, she began taking Hungarian lessons: now she's fluent and leads guided tours around Budapest. 'It's so brilliant to find that my brain hasn't atrophied. I'm never going to make self-deprecating jokes about senior moments again!'

Some people find new ways of using their experience. Bill retired from his job at a large engineering firm in 1995 at the age of 63. Since then he's done stints in the Philippines, Bolivia, Honduras and Sri Lanka, advising their governments on how to dispose of their waste in environmentally sound but cheap ways.

Work, though, isn't the only way of keeping mentally alert and engaged: there's also lifelong education. The University of the Third Age, in which each member both teaches and learns, maintains that 'there is no upper age limit on curiosity.' They argue that learning should be deeply pleasurable and need never stop. Indeed many of us only learn how to really learn when we're older.

Another received idea about ageing is the belief that we become more conservative as we age. Analysis of recent voting patterns, though, suggests that older voters are now more radical than younger ones. One older radical was the writer Olive Dehn. In 1988, aged 74, she took the Central Electricity Generating Board to court for 'conspiring with the government to make plutonium to sell to the USA for the making of nuclear weapons.'

Joy in being

Of course, listing 'late achievements' like this can give the impression that older people must keep on frenetically 'doing' to defy the years and justify their existence. What's wrong with just sitting and staring? A friend of Marie de Hennezel described the pleasures of advanced old age. They included sitting on a bench and feeling the sun on his face: 'It is . . . being more internally and doing less externally.' No wonder cultures where being is devalued and doing over-valued regard old age with such contempt and dread! If some older people's continuing attainments and passions are turned into the norm to which we all must aspire – a blueprint for ageing 'well' – then they become horribly counterproductive. The whole point about ageing 'well' is to be able to say, as the American poet May Sarton did when she turned 70, 'Why is it good to be old? Because I am more myself than I have ever been.'

This liberation from social expectation comes up again and again in older people's descriptions of the pleasures of ageing: what opens up is the possibility of caring less what other people want for or from you, and more about your own sense of 'rightness'. Says Rachel, 74,

> When I was younger I was either a daughter, a wife or a mother. I have discovered myself in the last twenty-five years – what my strengths are, what I like to do. Sometimes it's all right to put yourself first. I work for the Samaritans – and that work takes precedence over the grandchildren, unless there's a crisis. I've got involved in a theatrical thing put on by Age UK – I've never done anything theatrical in my life before, but now I think, is there a side of me that's never been explored?

But save us from 'eccentricity'

Yet individuality in old people seems to excite a stereotype all of its own, in which they're cast in the role of 'eccentric'. Jenny Joseph's poem, 'Warning' – the one that begins 'When I am an old woman I shall wear purple' – is the most famous example. First published in 1961, this supposedly inspiring image of old age has been taken up as an anthem over the past twenty years by baby boomers anxious about ageing. You can now buy it emblazoned on purple T-shirts, tote bags, and even snack trays. Yet it's whimsical, patronizing, and stereotyping. Better by far the many internet parodies it's inspired,

Individuality in old people seems to excite a stereotype all of its own, in which they're cast in the role of 'eccentric'.

most of them by men, e.g. 'When I'm an old man I shall wear false teeth, and wear hearing aids'. And young women can't wear purple?

The search for meaning

Human beings wouldn't reach 70 or 80, the psychoanalyst Carl Jung believed, if such longevity had no meaning for the species. 'The afternoon of human life must also have a significance of its own and cannot be merely a pitiful appendage to life's morning.' And if there's a single preoccupation that drives people from midlife onwards, it's this search for meaning in their lives; the midlife crisis – if indeed such a thing exists – could be said to be a crisis of meaning. It leads us to question how we've lived our lives so far – whether we've lived the way we thought we ought, rather than as we truly wished – and sometimes make radical changes.

So ageing has the potential to become an alchemical process, the agent of change, throughout life. In *Ikiru*, the 1952 expressionist masterpiece by the Japanese film director Akira Kurosawa, the hero is an ageing civil servant who is barely alive. When he is diagnosed with stomach cancer, he feels impelled to have a last stab at living. Through a series of encounters, including one with a young and ultimately insensitive young colleague, he finds a purpose for his final months, and dies more alive than he's ever been. Although Kurosawa was only 42 when he made the film, it was driven by his doubts about the value of his own life. 'I keep feeling I have lived so little. My heart aches with the feeling.' The film provided an answer: even in the pall of imminent death, a new meaning can be discovered in life.

Psychological growth, it turns out, can take place at any stage in the life course – and all through it. Old age, May Sarton insisted, isn't a fixed point 'any more than sunrise or sunset or the ocean tide. At every instant the psyche is in flux.' She believed that at 70 she was better able to use her abilities. She was also surprised to feel not the detachment which she'd assumed would come with age but the opposite – attachment, with the ability to live more fully in the moment. 'I am happy because I feel alive and well and in a constant state of expectation before each day . . . the joys of my life have nothing to do with age. They do not change. Flowers, the morning and evening light, music, poetry, silence, the goldfinches darting about . . .'

Less is more

The British politician Denis Healey found that, as he aged, 'psychologically I have widened.' He became more interested in people, more sensitive to colour, music and sunlight and loved his family more. 'I have lost all my interest in power and position and no longer worry about making money.' This is a common theme, especially among men who were inordinately work-focused when they were younger. What's often called 'burnout' may, in fact, be some visceral sense that life has got out of kilter; it's a self-protective mechanism. Since the demands of work have become more intense and unrelieved in those who have jobs, it's not surprising that we're burning out younger and younger: now, it seems, women below the age of 30 with demanding jobs are suffering burnout just like men. As they move into their thirties, they may have to learn how to convert some of their blistering energy into staying power.

When we talk about life shrinking as we age what may actually be happening is this sloughing off of inessentials. As the French actress Nathalie Baye put it when she was 63, 'That's the trick about ageing: you need to somehow become lighter at the same time.' Lighter can mean not spreading oneself so thinly, mono-tasking rather than multi-tasking, learning to say no.

Yet in order to do this we may have to let go of a lifetime's obsessions and grievances. Middle age and beyond provides an opportunity to look back over our lives and grieve for the good things that never happened and the bad that did – to work through pain, loss and unresolved conflicts and let them go, rather than dragging them around behind us like an increasingly heavy suitcase.

And so we come back to mourning again. Some losses are particularly hard to mourn – the death of a partner after forty years together, for example. Or the death of one's friends and the ensuing solitude. Or the loss of mobility. And yet the psychoanalyst Danielle Quinodoz gives dozens of examples of old people she's either met or treated who were able to let go of all these things after periods of deep sadness and who felt freer after mourning what they'd lost.

When Lou, an 80-year-old widow crippled by osteoarthritis, moved into a care home she transformed the atmosphere by creating a climate of conviviality: she organized word games, recounted her own memories and listened to other people's. The residents all became more animated and interested in each other as a result. Lou's experience persuaded Quinodoz that it's possible to lose almost everything without losing oneself. This is a remarkably encouraging view of growing older, but one which never slides over into sentimentality, or the denial of pain. It reminds us that, ultimately, pain can be modified by optimism and love. Why is this so hard to remember?

Still loving, after all these years

It's self-evident that those people who retain their capacity for love and affection find ageing easier, but what often gets obscured is that this ability need never stop developing. There's no evidence that we love less, or love fewer people, as we age. Although the capacity to love is established in infancy, in response to the care we're given, Erikson argued that, once a person has established their own identity, they are more capable of creating intimate, reciprocal relationships. What's more, as we age we find other ways of expressing love instead of, or in addition to, sexual ones. You can't replace a beloved person who dies, but you can continue to find other people to love.

W. H. Auden said 'We must love one another or die'. Of course we die anyway, but more peacefully if we've loved.

Those with an aptitude for gratitude also find ageing easier: they relish what they still have. Diana Athill's books are so delicious because they're so wholly without self-pity: she simply accepts the fact of ageing and some of the losses it inevitably brings, as well as her earlier life, with all its pleasures and pains. Even as she moves into residential care, Athill never loses sight of all the good things in her life, and her capacity to appreciate and savour them doesn't falter. What a wonderful talent – to be able to accept ageing, but resist the limitations imposed by ageism.

A 100-year-old woman, when she was interviewed on radio, was asked if she had any regrets. 'If I'd known I'd live to be 100', she replied, 'I'd have taken up the violin at 40. By now I could have been playing for 60 years!'

4. Between the Ages

When caricatures of old people seem not just tenacious but also inevitable – this is when we need to turn to history. But if we don't idealize the past, are we really going to feel happier about growing older by learning that the ancient Sardinians hurled their elders off high cliffs, and roared with laughter when they fell onto the rocks below? Or that in remote parts of Japan adults used to eat old men once they'd reached a certain age? Perhaps the point of such grisly accounts is to make us appreciate that, with our heating allowance and free NHS prescriptions to look forward to (always assuming these survive), ours is going to be a pampered ageing, so we should shut up and quit complaining.

No: what history shows us is that attitudes towards old people can and have changed – even if not invariably for the better; there's nothing immutable or 'natural' about them. The more we learn about the historical origins of ageism, the easier it is not to take it personally.

As Simone de Beauvoir pointed out, 'a man's [sic] ageing and his decline always takes place inside some given society.' Looking back and elsewhere reveals how much our opinions and behaviour are shaped by the societies we live in and, even more, by their economies: what ends with a casual expression of ageism – 'he's showing his age' – begins with economic anxieties. Understand this and you have a whole trunk of tools to help combat ageism.

No golden age

Certainly gerontophobia has a long history. Aristotle called old people small-minded, malicious and ungenerous. Plautus practically invented the stereotype of the dirty but impotent old man. Senecide – the killing of old people – was common practise in many cultures. The Hopi abandoned their old in specially built huts. The Samoans buried their elders alive, while the Nambikwara Indians have one word meaning young and beautiful, and another for both old and ugly.

In most traditional societies you were shown respect only as long as you were socially useful. There were practical reasons for this: as the historian David Hackett Fischer pointed out, in groups living close to the edge of subsistence, dependent old people were a heavy burden on their kin. Indeed senecide often exists side by side with infanticide.

Old and powerful

Pre-industrial societies certainly weren't all gerontocracies, where old people ruled. Still, old age, when it was much rarer than now, had a scarcity value and was a far more venerated state: age often conferred prestige and privileges, power and authority. In ancient Greece you couldn't become a member of the jury until 50. The Roman Senate originated from the word *senex*, meaning aged. Between 1400 and 1600, the average age of the doges, who held the highest office in the Venetian republic, was 72.

Although early modern Europeans searched obsessively for the Fountain of Youth, the idea that older meant worse was foreign. In the seventeenth century men wore wigs powdered white because they wanted to look old. In eighteenth century New England, people tried to make themselves seem older than they actually were by adding years to their real age, rather than subtracting them.

The big shift

But the nineteenth century saw the start of a profound change in the way old age was thought about: the idea that ageing was part of the human condition, with its inevitable limits, increasingly gave way to a conception of old age as a biomedical problem to which there might be a scientific solution.

This was reflected in changes to both customs and language. In seventeenth-century America the best seats in meeting houses were reserved for old people. Between 1770 and 1840 they lost those privileged seats, yielding them to the wealthy, and new laws forced them to retire at a fixed age. Before 1780 'fogey' meant a wounded military veteran; by 1830 it had acquired the meaning it has today – a pejorative term for an old, hidebound person. Similarly 'senile' was transformed in the nineteenth century from a value-free adjective signifying old age to a medical term conveying the debilitations of old age, most often paired with 'dementia'. 'Codger', 'superannuated' and eventually 'geriatric' joined them in the lexicon of contempt for the old.

However, most words that describe older women never had such salad days: 'hag' and 'crone', like almost every term of abuse

Before 1780 'fogey' meant a wounded military veteran.

combining old with female, have a long history. 'Old maid', even in the sixteenth century, was disparaging, while 'witch' invariably attributed a dangerous power to older women. 'Spinster' is the exception. Originally it meant a woman who spun wool, a rare occupation open to women, which enabled them to make a living independent of a man. Today, though, it's a derogatory term, used to refer to all older, single women, and which implies that they haven't been able to find a husband rather than chosen not to marry.

It's easy to overstate this change – in reality, attitudes to older people have always varied enormously, and so have their experiences. And of course definitions of age change over time. When the average lifespan in the middle ages was vastly shorter than today, it's hardly surprising that to the poet Dante old age began at 46.

Yet in the nineteenth century 'the aged' came to be seen as a distinct social group, segregated from the rest of society. You were now less likely to become a pauper as you aged, but at the same time you were less likely to be respected. Before the big shift, older people were seen as playing a vital social role. After it, although their medical and economic conditions improved, their social importance declined.

Thomas Cole, another historian of old age, has argued that by the late nineteenth century, middle-class Protestantism – the dominant culture – had lost the ability to face ageing with 'existential integrity', replacing it instead with fear, evasion and hostility towards old people.

The emerging idea that humans were perfectible brought with it a belief that the precariousness of life could be eradicated, and that human limits need no longer apply. Old age became a disease, a pathology demanding special professional expertise, if not custodial care. What got lost, Cole suggests, was any framework that made sense – morally, spiritually or metaphysically – of growing old. Ageing needed to be 'managed', and was split between 'good' ageing and 'bad'. Cole has talked of the 'de-meaning of later life.' Interestingly it was just at this point in the nineteenth century, when old age was coming to be devalued, that sentimental Victorian images of old age emerged. Sanctimonious attitudes towards older people seem to have developed almost as a cover for the loss of respect and role.

The result is a whole set of illogical attitudes to old people. For instance, although we're living longer, fitter and healthier lives than ever before, we spend more time worrying about ageing: we get older later but fear getting older younger. This is particularly strange since technology has made brute strength less important. You'd imagine that, as a result, there'd be less prejudice against older people who are physically weaker than younger ones. Yet while ageing, argues the gerontologist Alan Walker, is a dynamic process and is changing all the time, public policy is locked into the past and lags behind lived experience by at least twenty years. This 'structural lag', as he calls it, prevents older people playing their full part in society.

Why did attitudes towards old people change so much? In 1972 a pair of social scientists, Donald Cowgill and Lowell Holmes, put forward a 'modernization theory'. They argued that old people had higher status in preliterate societies than in modern industrialized states, where individual achievements were emphasized at the expense of the group.

Other researchers disagreed, insisting that the status of older people declined *before* modernization, and that we shouldn't be misled by the public veneration of old people in the past: often, in private, people voiced rather less salubrious sentiments. And anyway, whatever people said and wrote, if you were old and poor in pre-industrial times your life was likely to be pretty abject.

Still others claim that it wasn't industrialization that made us less respectful towards older people but new ideas of social equality: why should one group deserve more reverence than any other? Yet urbanization and industrialization have undoubtedly had a major effect on attitudes towards ageing, even if the biggest shift happened a hundred years later, in the twentieth century.

Old wasn't always old-fashioned

It's hard to believe that, in the 1940s and 1950s, young people wanted to look older than they were. *Parents* magazine in 1956 featured clothing for adolescents: the models and the styles of suit they wore make them look 40 to us now.

The journalist Katharine Whitehorn recalls borrowing her aunt's dress for a Cambridge May ball in 1947: 'who would borrow an aunt's garment now? . . we aspired to the same clothes as adults . . . it seems another world.'

In the 1940s *Vogue* introduced a character called Mrs Exeter (in the form first of drawings and later a model) to represent the older woman. What strikes sociologist Julia Twigg, who has studied ageing and dress, is how 'unrepentantly' old Mrs Exeter – with her white hair and restrained clothes (and pointedly married name) – seems to us now. In 1949 *Vogue* wrote 'Approaching 60, Mrs Exeter does not look a day younger, a fact she accepts with perfect good humour

Model Margot Smyly assumed the role of *Vogue*'s Mrs Exeter – with her white
hair, restrained clothes (and pointedly married name), she seems 'unrepentantly'
old to us now.

and reasonableness.' To modern ears she might as well have been a visitor from another galaxy.

Old as bitter, not better

Most historians agree that, whenever the decline in status of old people began, 'second modernity' – the period of continuing rapid social change that started in the late twentieth century – accelerated the process. Certainly you can see the emergence of a new geronto-phobia already in the youth culture of the 1960s, when popular music asked 'Will you still need me, will you still feed me, when I'm 64?' and proclaimed 'Hope I die before I get old' to a generation whose mantra was 'Never trust anyone over 30'.

Nothing enshrined these attitudes better than Mike Nichols's 1967 film *The Graduate*. Although Anne Bancroft was only 36 when she played the older woman, Mrs Robinson, she stands for everything that's sterile and repressive in middle-aged, bourgeois culture. The film takes brilliant aim at almost every cultural institution – marriage, business, the church and education – but its ageism seems to have passed unnoticed. Beautiful, bitter Mrs Robinson tries to make her daughter's life as attenuated as her own. In the glorious final church scene, just after Elaine has exchanged vows with the WASP (White Anglo-Saxon Protestant) husband they've picked out for her, the Robinsons look up at the bellowing Ben (Dustin Hoffman), their mouths contorted into a grotesque rictus of rage. Trying to stop Elaine escaping with him, Mrs Robinson barks at her: 'It's too late!' Retorts Elaine, 'Not for me.'

The Graduate: The Robinsons look up at the bellowing Ben (Dustin Hoffman), their mouths contorted into a grotesque rictus of rage.

Tainted by experience

Technology has transformed how we view old people. In slow-changing, traditional – predominantly oral – societies, elders were more likely to be valued because they transmitted knowledge, experience and indeed the history of the tribe to the next generation. Custodians of tradition, they could impart practical skills – everything from fishing to myths and songs – and continuity.

Today, in comparison, we suffer from what sociologist Richard Sennett calls 'skills extinction'. If you're an engineer, or even a lawyer, doctor or computer repairman, the skills that you learned in college no longer last a lifetime: skill isn't a durable asset or experience a virtue any more. (When John Drummond, Controller of Radio 3 and Director of the Proms, objected to a change in the BBC, an administrator accused him of being 'tainted by experience'.) It's far cheaper to buy in a young new employee than pay to retrain an older one. Perhaps it's not surprising, then, that anxieties about ageing that would have been regarded as pathological in the 1950s are today considered normal, as are the costly steps taken to counteract them.

We don't value older people for their memories, either, since we assume that technology is going to do the remembering for us. It's not just older people who are scared of 'getting left behind' – all of us are having to learn to live with long-term precariousness; we're all only as good as our last project. This kind of anxious, ruthless individualism pits younger against older, and encourages us to see everyone as our rival.

Other cultures

So where can we look for inspiration – China? There the Confucian idea of 'filial piety' – an elaborate code of obligations demanding respect, patience and support – is so powerful it's enshrined in law: Chinese adults are required to support their parents. Yet growing individualism, the fast pace of social change and the one-child policy, which places the responsibility of supporting two parents onto one child, are creating tensions. Young Chinese no longer feel the same respect for older people that their parents did.

What about Japan? In the mid-twentieth century it was seen as the older person's nirvana. Compared to other industrial societies, Japanese old people enjoyed higher status, were more integrated into society, and were more likely to live with and see their children. There 'filial piety' combined with ancestor worship to create a deferential, paternalistic country. The most common word for old people in Japan was *otoshiyori* – 'the honourable elders'.

Today young Japanese are increasingly ambivalent about their elders. They've coined a new phrase: *kaigo-jigoku* – the 'care-giving hell' of those who look after their relatives. Elder abuse is increasing and, although a high percentage over-65s still live with their children, social security now does much of the work that filial piety did before.

All this is conveyed poignantly in Yasujiro Ozu's screen masterpiece, *Toyko Story* (1953), in which an elderly couple make the long journey from their home to visit their children in Tokyo. Neither their hairdresser daughter nor their doctor son have time for them, paying for them to go to a noisy spa instead, and their youngest son, who lives outside Toyko, is equally nonchalant. Only their widowed daughter-in-law, Noriko, treats them with love and respect. *Tokyo Story* is a melancholy portrait of the Japanese family in the throes of transition and 'modernization', as filial piety was turning from a daily practice into an abstract concept.

And *otoshiyori*? Today it's increasingly used ironically.

Young vs old

Christopher Buckley's satirical novel *Boomsday* opens with a TV news reporter covering a violent demonstration in Florida. Several hundred people in their twenties have stormed the gates of a 'retirement community', assaulting residents as they play golf. The target of their wrath is the nation's 77 million baby boomers who, retiring on lavish pensions, are placing an intolerable strain on the American economy. They line up to support a young woman's suggestion that the government give 75-year-olds incentives to kill themselves.

Outlandish, maybe, and a modern version of Trollope's *The Fixed Period*, but the idea of young people rioting in hostility to old people seems rather less far-fetched today than in 2008 when the novel was first published and is the ultimate reversal of the veneration of older people.

Indeed the concept of intergenerational inequality has never been as prominent as it is today. In his recent book, *The Pinch*, David Willetts, Conservative MP and Minister for Universities and Science, argued that baby boomers have concentrated wealth in the hands of their own rich and powerful generation, so ensuring that young people will have to pay more taxes, work longer for less pay, won't be able to afford to buy a house and will be left with an exorbitant level of national debt.

(Curiously he makes no mention of the fact that the government of which he's a part, indeed his very own ministry, dramatically increased university tuition fees, thereby preventing today's university students from enjoying the free higher education that he did.)

Again and again we find commentators evoking images of the greedy old, hogging jobs and houses and holding on tightly to businesses and assets, instead of letting these flow down to younger people in a generational transfer of wealth such as took place in earlier times.

This line of thought pits Us against Them and sees public policy as a zero-sum game: whatever They get leaves less for Us. Indeed pensions are characterized as a kind of Ponzi pyramid scheme, with the already-depleted current young having to shell out for the current old, without any prospect of it ever being reciprocated.

Older people are cast in a catch-22. If they retire early on a pension, they're leeching off the young; if they continue to work beyond retirement age, they're siphoning away jobs from young people. If they buy big houses they're inflating the housing bubble; if they downsize to smaller properties they're taking houses that should rightly go to young families. Free TV licences, winter fuel benefits – it's jam today, paid for by a generation that can expect jam never.

There's even a bespoke body, the Intergenerational Foundation, that exists 'to protect the rights of younger and future generations in British policymaking' (presumably against rapacious oldies). It publishes an annual Intergenerational Fairness Index, which logs how far the position of the younger generation is worsening.

But this is binary thinking at its most dangerous. It fuels geronto-phobia, and aggravates old people's already hefty fears of becoming a burden. And it does no favours to young people either, making it even harder for them to identify with older people, seeding an anxiety about getting older and becoming burdensome themselves, and generally positioning them as angry toddlers, having a tantrum because they're not getting what they want and think they're due.

What's worse, it plays into the current polarized 'scrounger' discourse of 'skivers' and 'strivers'. In the past, older people seemed safely beyond the reach of discussions about the 'deserving' and 'un-deserving' poor. But increasingly now, argues gerontologist Alan Walker, there's an attempt to identify them with the 'undeserving poor'.

The housing and employment prospects of young people today are undoubtedly grim, but the concept of 'intergenerational in-equity' – a term that originated in the United States in the 1980s from concerns that the pensions of an increasingly ageing popula-tion would prove unaffordable – rests on a fundamental distortion: that of a baby boomer generation which is uniformly wealthy. In reality, of course, old people and even 'new' pensioners include some of the poorest people in our society. While some of this cohort made a lot of money on the property market or through shares, an awful lot of them didn't, just as there are many young people doing well financially today, although most of them aren't.

It's the economy, stupid, and the political structure that deter-mines who benefits and who doesn't; social classes infinitely more than age-groups hoard social assets for their own. Similarly it was a political ideology, Thatcherism – rather than everyone who happened to be alive in the 1980s – that initiated the ideology of rolling back the state, continued by New Labour and accelerated by the current Conservative government.

The whole idea of 'generational accounting', a financial balance sheet of contributions and benefits drawn up throughout the life cycle, is challenged by sociologists Claudine Attias-Donfut and Sara Arber in *The Myth of Generational Conflict*. For example, the generation that took part in post-war reconstruction but may have paid relatively little in contributions: have they taken more than they've given? Or what about women who spent decades raising children? They may not have paid much income tax or National Insurance but have given years of unpaid labour to produce the next generation of citizens, as have those who care for the last one.

What's more, generational inequalities are only one type of inequality – much more modest, as Attias-Donfut and Arber point out, than inequalities based on class, gender and ethnicity. Yet rarely does the aggrieved young columnist who rails about their difficulty buying a flat devote equal column inches to households where poverty is multigenerational, or to the fact that women continue to earn significantly less than men.

In reality, the youngest *and* oldest members of society tend to be the poorest: far from dividing them, this is what they share. And when state benefits are given to the oldest members of a family, the advantages tend to trickle down to its other generations too. Interestingly, too, the countries that have the fewest inequalities between generations also have the fewest inequalities within them.

So why have these incorrect but harmful ideas about generational conflict flourished so much over the past few years? One reason is the slashing of public spending: when resources are limited, of course, competition over them increases, and with it comes the search for a scapegoat. State and public-sector pensions have also been caught up in the demonization of anything connected with public spending.

Age ghettoes

But there's another factor that has contributed to the virulence of the present debate – one which has particular bearing on our experience of growing older: age segregation. Apartheid may have been dismantled but age-apartheid has intensified. We've age-cleansed our society. Under the banner of welfare we've corralled old people into day-care centres and homes; removed them from families, schools, universities, workplaces, general-hospital wards and sports centres, creating age ghettoes. It might soon be perfectly possible to go through life without meeting an old person until you become one. No wonder the prospect of ageing is terrifying.

Perhaps we want older people removed from view because they stand as a permanent reminder that we too will get old and die? Author and activist Betty Friedan argued that people who could no longer 'pass' as young had to be quarantined lest they contaminate the rest of us.

Of course it's easy to dismiss nursing homes as segregationist – when you don't need them. Nor is this a plea for a return to the past, where 'daughter care' was taken for granted, and it was assumed that women's financial needs and aspirations should be sacrificed for the needs of older relatives. Until we're prepared to face up to our own ageing instead of seeing older people as taking what should be ours, it will be hard to have a proper national debate about the kinds of care for older people that most of us would wish for the people we love, and for ourselves.

Some older people choose to sequester themselves away from younger ones. Let's not forget 'retirement communities' – adult-only, child-free villages, where you're guaranteed never to meet anyone substantially younger than yourself. Why would you rule out other people purely on the basis of their age? Part of their appeal, some residents claim, is that they protect old people from the prejudice and discrimination of young people. Yet, insofar as they help the rest of us to deny our own ageing, they just make these worse.

Indeed young people's lack of contact with old people not only encourages them to believe that they'll never get old, but also to treat old people as if they'd never been young. This is especially easy to do in fast-moving societies where your degree of ease with social media, digital devices and apps seems to mark you out as a member of a younger age-cohort, although in reality it's not *because* you're young that you can swiftly master these widgets but because of *when* you're young. In the pre-internet era, technical skill wasn't a marker of youth. On the contrary, older people were more likely to have accumulated technical know-how. Particular abilities and beliefs aren't intrinsic to an age-group but to an era, and if that's when you're young and impressionable you're more likely to absorb them.

Yet we brand people as members of age-cohorts, among other things through 'generational marketing': special products and facilities for 'the old' and 'the young'. Some claim that these improve the quality of life, but their effect is to exile older and younger people in separate age Bantustans, rather than integrate them into the social world. Cinemas, for instance, often run special 'senior screenings' midmorning at a discounted rate, with free tea or coffee and biscuits. But mightn't unemployed young people appreciate these too?

The effects of age-segregation

There's a direct link between age segregation and ageism: when we don't encounter older people casually, regularly as part of our daily life, we screen them out of what gerontologist Bill Bytheway called our 'conceptual maps', too. Perhaps it's not surprising that three-quarters of the 84 Facebook groups, totalling 25,000 members, that used synonyms for 'old', 'aged' or 'elderly' examined in a recent study by the Yale School of Public Health were found to have vilified elderly people. Facebook expressly forbids hate speech directed at various groups, but older people are not among them. 'Everyone over the age of 69 should immediately face a firing squad' was typical of some of the comments posted. Created by 20- to 29-year-olds, more than one-third of these groups advocated banning older people from public activities like shopping.

Age segregation denies the fact that interests and preoccupations cross the ages: you can love reggae or oppose the renewal of Trident whatever your age – instead of age dividing us, passions can unite us. All the evidence – and there are banks of it – suggests that integrating the ages is transformative. If we have a wide range of age contacts, we stay vital and engaged for longer. And the more contact that young people have with older people, the more favourably they regard them, and the more positively they view their own ageing.

To challenge prejudice a recent American reality-TV series, *Forever Young*, thrust five under-thirties together with five over-seventies in a *Big Brother*-style house. By the end it was tears and mutual appreciation all round, despite the increasing frustration of the 'juniors' trying to induct the 'seniors' in new technology – 'Just click it!'

Research confirms that we judge older family members, like grandparents, in less stereotyped ways than older strangers. When Professor of English Kathleen Woodward taught a class on literature and ageing to American university students, she was struck by the way they split older people into two types. There were those they knew well, like grandparents and great-grandparents, whom they didn't see exclusively in terms of age – indeed sometimes their age didn't figure as important at all. Then there were those whom they didn't know personally, who were entirely subsumed beneath the label and stereotypes of 'old'.

Inter-age

We hear a lot about generational discord and jealousy, but far less about inter-generational solidarity, despite the emergence of some fabulous initiatives. Generations United, for instance, is an American organization trying to stimulate intergenerational collaboration. It runs a Best Intergenerational Communities award – a telling contrast to the Intergenerational Fairness Index.

Magic Me, the leading British organizer of intergenerational projects, links young people aged 8-plus with adults aged 60-plus in creative activities – music, dance, photography, printmaking, drama – as well conversation and an exchange of ideas. As one head teacher said, the young people involved 'begin to realize what they can learn from other generations.' Among its projects are Cocktails in Care Homes, monthly evening cocktail parties for residents of homes in East London. Through this initiative, a volunteer remarked, one resident 'has now relearnt the art of conversation.'

Art Cart, an American intergenerational arts project, links graduate students with ageing professional artists. The students help the professionals prepare and document their work, gaining valuable educational experience in the process. Homeshare programmes around the world introduce older homeowners who'd value company and assistance to younger people threatened with homelessness. In the USA 'cyber-grandparents', aged 60 to 105, are supplied by the Elder Wisdom Circle to provide anonymous advice to people in their twenties and thirties. Berlin has opened Europe's first multigenerational housing project for lesbian, gay, bisexual and transgender people.

When the Crosstalk project brought together children and old people in small towns in Italy and Germany to talk about the games and toys each had played with, the children were surprised at how mischievous the older people had been. After the project ended, they greeted the older people by name whenever they saw them. The older people were no longer a generic category: they'd become individuals with a real past and childhoods with which the children could identify.

Inter-generational friendship

But while organized schemes and projects like this have an important role to play, equally mind-shifting are informal cross-age friendships. Most of us today fraternize mainly with our age-peers, and while there are all sorts of stage-of-life things that are best shared with them, it's also limiting – as though you've never got over the propaganda dispensed when we're at school, where age is seen as the great definer, and people are either 'above' or 'below' you. (Michael Young, the sociologist who helped found the Open University, claimed that our age-stratified culture resembled a caste society: the one we're born into we have to stay with throughout our lives.)

For Lucy, a 63-year-old teacher, this started to change in her late twenties. 'First I met someone in his seventies at a demonstration and became friendly with him and his wife. Then I met a couple of women much older than me – one in her late seventies, the other in her early eighties. And we were so alike! It was great to become friends with people my parents' age, but who didn't share their politics or opinions – they made me realize that I wouldn't have to give up mine as I aged. Now I've got friends who are older and who are much younger, and I find it exciting to mix them up. I'd say the age span of my friends is around forty years.'

This only works, though, if you've accepted your own stage of the life cycle, and aren't too envious of younger people or triumphant towards older ones. Carola, 68, says, 'My life has improved enormously as I've got older, so I don't envy my younger friends, though I'm impressed at how much better they manage their lives than I did when I was their age. I think – I hope – that in me they have

Maitri House, an example of intergenerational community in Maryland, USA.

someone who makes them less scared of ageing. That's certainly what my older friends do for me.'

The writer Diana Athill maintains that contact with younger people can counter a tendency towards pessimism in old age. Watching a younger person at the beginning of their life is not only interesting, she argues, but reminds us not to waste our time complaining. For Shirley, a member of the older women's network the Hen Co-op, her sons, their partners, her younger women friends and the students with whom she's worked 'have taught me to loosen my sexual inhibitions, to have greater tolerance to those I do not understand.'

The Gray Panthers, founded in 1972 by Maggie Kuhn, believed in a coalition of young and old. 'When I think of all the children who have little meaningful contact with old people,' wrote Kuhn, 'I fear for the world.' Young people living in stress-filled homes with striving parents, she believed, needed the time and deeper perspective of older people. Yet with growing anxiety about paedophilia, opportunities for contacts between older people and younger have probably shrunk more than ever.

Kuhn herself lived inter-generationally. From her seventies until her death at 89, she shared her house in Philadelphia with young housemates. She wasn't, she insisted, a parent figure to them, nor did she patronize them. 'I like to talk to them about my life and listen to them talk about theirs ... By talking to people in their sixties, seventies and eighties, young people can get a sense that bad times come and go, that history and large social forces play a part in their personal dramas, and that life is finite.'

But cross-age friendships and working partnerships don't just mean an alliance of the very young and the very old: they're about opening yourself to relationships across the age span, so that one's friendship group includes people of all ages – young, adolescent, young adult, middle-aged and old. This helps develop our sense of ourselves as constantly changing, and our understanding that we can find kindred spirits of every age, at every age. Such relationships are a wonderful way of dispelling the rigid ideas with which we've been inculcated about what happens, or is supposed to, at each stage in life. Seeing people of all ages as potential friends requires a radical switch in thinking. But by nurturing friendships across the life cycle, we begin to understand that we can learn from, and be inspired by, people at any age. Embracing people of different ages is another way of embracing the ageing process itself.

Racial segregation now seems to most people reactionary and stupid. In a few decades' time, if people of all ages are fully integrated into public and private institutions and communal life, will age segregation strike us as similarly archaic and idiotic?

5. Age and Gender

Time to drop in again on Gina's parents, Sara and Clive. Sara isn't quite as sanguine about getting older as she was when we last saw her. She's gained some weight, which she thinks is ageing, and has started to worry that wearing her skirts short makes her look like 'mutton dressed as lamb'. But then she wonders if sheep are an entirely female species, since Clive and his mates happily wear the same T-shirts and chinos as their 20-something sons and never fret about their resemblance to meat. Sara is contemplating having a facelift – only because, she says, she thinks she looks permanently 'tired', and wants how she feels inside ('I don't feel old') to match her outside ('but I'm beginning to look it').

His and hers

Is Sara suffering from what Susan Sontag, in a major essay published in 1972, called 'the double standard about ageing'? Sontag argued that a woman's birth date was her dirty secret. Getting older, she claimed, was 'less profoundly wounding' for a man than it was for a woman because, for women, beauty was always identified with youthfulness. Older women, therefore, wanted to continue to look like girls, since those who could 'pass' as younger were still admired. But the bodies of old women who couldn't were regarded as obscene.

The result of all this, Sontag suggested, was that women became 'sexually ineligible' much earlier than men: if a man were widowed in his forties or fifties he almost invariably went on to remarry someone younger, but this was rarely possible for women. And women, she lamented, acquiesced in it all, ending up full of self-hatred.

Sontag was clearly addressing her own anxieties – those of a classically beautiful woman approaching 40 (her essay was published four months before her birthday). She was prey to almost pathological anxieties about ageing, many of them social in origin, but others personal to her. She also seemed not to notice her own ageism.

Yet she made important observations about the gendered nature of ageing. How true are they forty years later? And do they give us any help in the business of ageing? In answer to the first question, over the intervening four decades the experience of ageing for women and men has become worse, better and different – all at the same time.

Worse because, in an era that's so obsessed with the body and so permeated with visual images, appearance has assumed unprecedented importance. We're now expected to scrutinize, discipline and beautify our bodies throughout the life course – you're never too old to improve yourself, and never too young to start.

Although this often dresses itself up as a question of health, pull off its outer layers and underneath you find a preoccupation with youthfulness. What would an old, disabled but healthy and beautiful body look like? It's a question we can't answer today because those qualities seem mutually incompatible – that's why the 'but' is there.

Of course stereotyping and prescriptive ideas about gender limit us at every age. A large survey of women conducted by a fashion company in 2011 came up with something it called 'Midlife Mirror

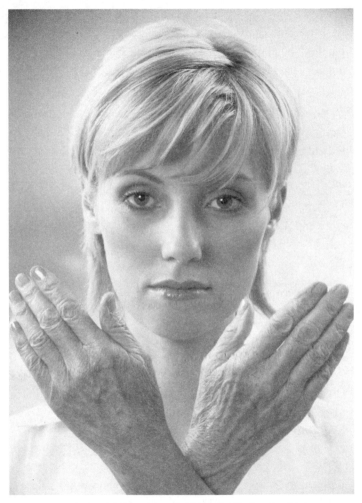

Oh the hands, the hands! They're regarded by beauty blogs and articles as a treacherous part of the body, divulging their owner's true age.

Angst': women who were so uncomfortable with their reflection that they avoided it. Just 9 per cent of those over 50 felt happy with what they saw in the mirror, compared with 43 per cent of 20-somethings. It's hard to decide which of those two percentages is the more depressing. Whichever, it suggests that the majority of women are unhappy about the way they look.

With help from the press, cinema, advertising and the internet, women have learned down the years to objectify themselves, to see their bodies as something separate from their self – something that could 'betray' them if they don't placate it with anti-ageing products. Oh the hands, the hands! They're regarded by beauty blogs and articles as a treacherous part of the body, which has broken ranks by divulging their owner's true age.

Trying not to age

Body dysmorphia – a distorted sense of one's body and appearance – used to be considered an individual psychological problem. Today it's become a cultural condition. Increasing numbers of middle-aged women now have the startled look caused by a facelift – as if they're puzzling to remember what they really look like.

The media are on permanent age-watch, with celebrities apparently fair game. Newspapers, magazines, websites and blogs monitor and police their appearance for signs of ageing, but also for signs of too much 'work' to conceal ageing. If they exhibit the normal signs of ageing, famous women look 'haggard', but if they take steps to combat it then the headlines sneer 'Ageing Cher is Losing her Battle to Turn Back Time' or 'Does Faye Dunaway Look a Little Ghoulish?' It's true that women – and men – who've resorted to the scalpel and dermal filler too obsessively look not young but just tragicomically afraid of growing old, but is this surprising?

Older women are at a disadvantage not only because they must strive to look permanently young. After a lifetime of earning less than men, or taking time out to raise children, they're also likely to be poorer. Far more women over 50 than men have become unemployed since 2010. And older women are most likely to make up the 'sandwich' or 'pivot' generation, who care for the youngest and oldest members of their family at the same time. It's enough to give anyone worry lines.

Young and anxious

Yet what's especially dispiriting is that young women too are now starting to worry about ageing. They see it entirely in terms of appearance, and regard it as a kind of looming disaster. A skincare company which surveyed a large number of them found that they become anxious about 'losing their looks' at around 28. Cosmetics brands, of course, encourage this by producing protective 'serums' designed for those aged 25-plus and stronger ones in the same range for 30-year-olds. Walmart has even introduced a skincare line, Geo-Girls, for 'tweens' – 8- to 12-year-old girls – with cosmetics, and 'anti-ageing' creams containing antioxidants. Since these could clog their pores and increase their skin's sensitivity to sun, they may in fact be damaging rather than protective.

And always there are the anxious celebrities to collude with these trends. Scarlett Johansson started using anti-ageing products at 20 and actress Charice Pempengco, to look fresh-faced for her role in *Glee*, had Botox at 18. Young women are drenched with news and images of these stars, so it's hardly surprising that they take in a powerful message about age. A 16-year-old from Oxford told the *Independent* in 2005, 'There is definite pressure on us as young people not to look old but to try to look 18, and to stay looking that age even when you are well past it.' A 17-year-old was blunter: 'I don't want to be 50 and look gross.' So Sontag wasn't far wrong when she identified the girl's body as the template.

Which star today would resist having her photos touched up, as Audrey Helpburn did, with the words, 'No, I've earned these lines!'

The causes

The denigration of older women has a long history. Freud wrote in 1913 that:

> It is well-known, and has been a matter for much complaint, that women alter strangely in character after they have abandoned their genital functions. They become quarrelsome, peevish, and argumentative, petty and miserly; in fact they display sadistic and anal-erotic traits which were not theirs in the era of womanliness. Writers of comedy and satirists have in all ages launched their invective against the 'old termagant' into which the sweet maiden, the loving woman, the tender mother, has deteriorated.

Thanks, Sig.

Of course there's money to be made out of pathologizing ageing. The pharmaceutical industry, for instance, has found the medicalization of the menopause extremely lucrative. Today, in Western countries, we think of menopause almost entirely in relation to problems like hot flushes, or increased risks – of osteoporosis, heart disease, stroke – for which medication like hormone replacement therapy is routinely prescribed. But this perspective isn't universal. The menopause is viewed quite differently in Japan, for instance, where it isn't seen as a marker of midlife: hot flushes are barely reported (do Japanese women not have them, or not notice them?) and, if there are any 'symptoms' of the menopause, they're – curiously – stiff shoulders.

Researchers Margaret Lock and Patricia Kaufert suggest that this is partly because Japanese women have a different diet from Western women. But their other explanation is more intriguing: so many Japanese women still live in three-generational households that, they suggest, their fifties are seen as the prime of their lives, when they're at the acme of responsibility. This endows the menopause with a different meaning from that in Western countries, and reveals how much our experience of this stage in the life cycle is shaped by the culture we live in.

The anxious older man

Clive might not be going through the menopause but this doesn't mean that he's untouched by concerns about getting older. Indeed, the opposite is true: for a while now he too has been beset by a creeping sense of anxiety. There's a new egalitarianism abroad: what was confined to women has today spread to men, with age stigmatized in *both* of them.

Clive's anxiety was triggered when he read that Gordon Ramsay, at the age of 41, had had the deep crevasses in his forehead and chin plumped out with filler. Clive always thought his own lines and greying hair made him look 'distinguished', but he's noticed a growing number of his colleagues of the same age resorting to the chemical and surgical procedures they'd always dismissed as women's territory. They reason that, in the world of business start-ups, especially digital ones, you need to emit a sense of dynamism and, well, grey hair and wrinkles suggest the opposite. Clive is seriously wondering whether to follow suit.

A plethora of products and services tailored for men are now on offer, from 'regrowth formulae' for baldness to a 'new anti-age system engineered for men to keep skin looking younger' ('system' and 'engineered' making it sound properly un-feminine). 'We live in a culture of facial discrimination,' a cosmetic surgeon told the *Evening Standard* in 2009, 'and especially if you work in the City, you are judged on how you look. It is no longer the case that wrinkles and grey hair [in men] represent experience.' 'Last year,' said another surgeon, 'we saw many men who had been made redundant, or who thought they might lose their jobs, who wanted to look better and younger and to be able to compete with the younger guys in the industry.'

Older men have now joined older women as objects of disgust. The ageing rock star is invariably described as 'grizzled' and the music he makes 'colostomy rock'. Tina Turner's vigorous performing

Paul Newman in his sixties: A man with greying hair used to be regarded as distinguished

elicits admiration, yet Mick Jagger doing the same earns contempt. And will the sexual older man ever lose the prefix 'dirty'? The arrival of Viagra has only reinforced this description, confirming them as unreconstructed priapics and libertines. Though what it really demonstrates is precisely the opposite: that male sexuality can be a fragile thing. But then understanding this would require us to put aside too many easy prejudices.

Indeed in some sense men have been damaged by the arrival of Viagra, because it encourages them to see their younger selves as the benchmark against which their older sexuality must be compared, and which they must try to recover pharmaceutically. For if older women are invariably judged by their younger beauty, so older men are always assessed by their younger vigour. Whether you're a man or a woman, you're not supposed to change, or to enjoy your older self.

Yet if we were more able to have a less sneering and jeering debate about older men and sex, more of them might savour their gentler and slower sexuality, and even discover that their partners find it more erotic.

Fighting back

With rising divorce rates older men as well as women are 'dating' again, and both feel under pressure to present a groomed appearance. Ordinary people are increasingly having to try to meet standards of airbrushed looks that were formerly only expected of the young and famous. It's easy to understand why we feel flattered when told that we don't look our age. But basking in compliments like these brings only short-term relief. In the long term they're dangerous: they only allow us to defer our discomfort until the time when we do look our age.

This doesn't mean that everyone is equally susceptible to the pressure to deny ageing: those who question and challenge these norms are all around us. Like Barbara, a member of the older women's network, the Hen Co-op:

> We have been conditioned to look at our own bodies through the lens of the advertiser's camera. But I have come to see my old woman's body as beautiful in its own way. The full breasts which fed my children . . . the arms that have worked and nurtured and comforted. Now I fit my own body, I no longer long for it to be different. We should learn not to compare our bodies or devalue them or look at them through other people's eyes.

Barbara has found a way of actively resisting the imprecations of the beauty industry, and she's not alone.

The classicist Mary Beard, whenever she appears on television, has her appearance savaged on social media by trolls. Retorts Beard, 'Grey is my hair colour. I really can't see why I should change it. There clearly is a view of female normative behaviour but more women of 58 do look like me than like Victoria Beckham.'

Not all Western women, either, see menopause as a problem to which hormone replacement therapy is the solution. Lucy, 63, recalls:

> I barely noticed my menopause. I don't feel smug about it as I've got friends who did have a hard time. My life was just

so demanding, with work and children and so on, I didn't have time to think about it. They say you suffer mood swings, but I'm such a volatile person anyway you couldn't tell the difference. Since then I feel more sexually attractive and my business has taken off. I don't think these changes have got anything to do with the menopause either: I just know myself better and listen to myself more.

If only younger women could see that ageing might be like this.

Even among all the prejudice, there's cause for good cheer too. Because, increasingly, casual ageism and discrimination against older women – and men – is being named and challenged. By women like Beard and Miriam O'Reilly, who at 53 was axed from her job as presenter of TV's *Countryfile* in favour of a younger presenter, and took the BBC to a tribunal where she won an age-discrimination case. By the actresses Juliet Stevenson, Lesley Manville and Gemma Jones, who spoke out a few years back about the pressures on older actresses to look younger and the lack of parts written for them. By www.ageimmaterial.org, a British blog discussing issues affecting working women over 50, and 'Look at Me! Images of Women and Ageing Project', which challenges stereotypical representations of older women (www.representing-ageing.com), and many more.

Whenever grievances about the invisibility of older women are voiced, paradoxically they reveal how older women are becoming culturally more prominent. They're speaking out because they aren't prepared to withdraw from public life and debate purely on grounds of their age and gender. By drawing attention to the stereotyping of the older woman they're taking the first steps towards de-stigmatizing and reclaiming the ageing female body. And each time they do so they embolden someone else to reject the idea that ageing is their own personal shame, or that challenging gerontophobia is a hopeless task.

These aren't just uplifting slogans from the manual of positive thinking. Study any successful movement for social change and you'll find that it began with this process, of naming and un-shaming. And this is why things are better today than in 1972, when Sontag wrote her essay, even with the endless bile being pumped out by the cosmetics industry. For, back then, she was pretty much a lone voice.

Today, when Dove's Campaign for Real Beauty has used real women over 50, when the National Union of Journalists has helped draw up a charter to try to help raise awareness of the limited and damaging ways in which older women are represented in the media – then you know that change, albeit slow and incremental, is afoot, and that protests, debates and campaigns can have an impact. Participating in them can make you feel that you're not just the passive recipient of advertising, and remind you how many other people of every age reject insidious ageist propaganda.

The ageing heart

There's another respect in which things have improved and are improving. Increasingly, popular culture is recognizing that love is not the preserve of the young. The psychotherapist Marie de Hennezel argues that 'something within us does not grow old. I shall call it the heart. I don't mean the organ, which does of course age, but the capacity to love and desire. The heart I refer to is that inexplicable, incomprehensible force that keeps the human being alive, and which Spinoza christened *conatus*: primordial energy or vital endeavour.'

Carola is 68. She's certain that 'I'm far more able to love now than when I was in my twenties, thirties or even forties. I was too self-absorbed then to really be able to focus on another person. I was also pretty unforgiving. Now I'm just able to enjoy all the good things about my partner and feel grateful for them.'

Sex

Older women have been de-sexed for a long time, partly because we associate them with our mothers, with whom sex is taboo. But TV programmes like *Sex and the City*, with its sexually voracious character Samantha, signalled a change in attitude to older women's sexuality. Kim Cattrall, the actress who played her, insists that 'There is no age limit on sexuality'. Inevitably, perhaps, the mass media seized upon this issue of age and sex, and now every second newspaper or website, it seems, carries a story about a woman in her thirties or forties having sex with a younger man. Branded the 'cougar', she's been turned into a new stereotype and the butt of humour, as though a couple's respective ages were the most important thing about them.

Recent British research has discovered that, in reality, sexual relationships continue way beyond the stereotypes, with the majority of 50- to 90-year-olds sexually active. Maggie Kuhn famously urged widows to take younger lovers or have relationships with other women. In the Gray Panthers, she said, 'we hope that opportunities will be open to people of both sexes to establish deep friendships and loving relationships until rigor mortis sets in.' Kuhn herself had a sexual relationship with a 21-year-old man when she was 76.

Shirley, a member of the women's network the Hen Co-op, describes beautifully how her anxiety, in her late fifties, about exposing her body to a younger lover was slowly replaced by the pleasures of a satisfying sexual experience. And Carola, 68, thinks her sexual relationship is more intense now than when she was younger because she's more open, and less frightened of being overwhelmed by her feelings. Such women challenge the idea that sexuality is the prerogative of youth.

Perhaps we can learn from Mediterranean countries. Like France, where older women seem to be accorded longer sexual lives. It's common to see older Frenchwomen, as well as Spanish and Italian women, who look chic and comfortable in their skin, wrinkles and all, as if they hadn't realized that they were supposed to be put out to pasture. When someone asked the German Princess Palatine in the eighteenth century at what age sexual desire disappeared she replied, 'How should I know? I'm only 80.'

Or perhaps we should follow the advice of Agatha Christie. She recommended women marry an archaeologist, like she had, as he regarded a woman as more beautiful and interesting as she aged.

Changing sexualities

Ageing, as we've seen, involves both change and continuity. One interesting new phenomenon is that older people are no longer assuming that, just because a relationship is long-standing, if it's no longer fulfilling it needs to be endured. Increasing numbers of people in their fifties and sixties, for instance, are divorcing, sometimes after decades of marriage: often a birthday, or a brush with illness, causes them to ask 'is this all there is?' or 'do I still have time to develop a richer relationship?' There's even a new publishing genre, 'hen-lit', that fictionalizes the phenomenon. Many of these 'silver splitters', as they've been called, have turned into 'silver surfers' (the terms 'silver' and 'grey' are certainly getting a good workout these days) who are turning to online dating.

Others, after a lifetime of heterosexuality, find joy and sexual satisfaction in a same-sex relationship. And then there are those who, though they'd like to have a sexual relationship, can't find one. Some are resourceful. Jane Juska put an ad in the *New York Review of Books* that read 'Before I turn 67, next March, I would like to have a lot of sex with a man I like. If you want to talk first, Trollope works fine.'

There's always the danger, though, that sex in old age becomes the new norm – compulsory, rather than freely chosen. Yet many women identify with the writer Diana Athill, for whom sex was central in her earlier years, but who experienced a falling-away of desire with equanimity and without regret. Some feel relieved to be free of the anxiety of sexual encounters: after a lifetime of attending to the needs of others, they're only too grateful to be able to put their own needs first as they age, and relish the pleasures of being on their own. And let's celebrate those women who delight in the freedoms brought by age and give themselves permission to wear elasticated waistbands and sensible shoes, comfort finally triumphing over fashion.

For you can't repeat it too often: we become more different from one another as we age, and not less. There is no template for ageing, or ageing well. The best way is one's own way.

And love

Sex has so hijacked public discussion that it often squeezes out the many different kinds of love besides sexual. And yet the possibilities of different kinds of love, and different ways of loving, can widen as we age. Grandparents, for example, report themselves surprised by the ferocity – and tenderness – of their feelings for their grandchildren.

Increasingly, also, men and women are coming to see that too much has been expected of sexual relationships, and that, as they age, loving, close friendships can be equally, if not more, sustaining. The women's movement has made it more possible for women to feel kinship with each other, and not see other women as just rivals. Of course it hasn't eradicated competitiveness and envy, but it's allowed women to savour loving and non-sexual – as well as sexual – friendships with other women, and to create networks of support that can last until they die. The first British Older Women's Cohousing project, set to open in 2015, is a creative new way of maintaining independence while also combating isolation: its first residents, currently aged between 50 and 84, will own or rent their own flat but also have communal areas and will look out for each other.

So, although in some respects ageing has become even harder for women since Susan Sontag wrote about the double standard, especially since anxieties seem to set in now at an increasingly young age, in other respects it's become easier, with more women drawing attention to stereotypes and discrimination. What's also changed since Sontag's essay is that, increasingly, older men too are feeling the effects of ageist prejudice. Perhaps, in time, it will be widely recognized that men and women are both damaged by stereotypes of ageing, even if they're different ones. Maybe we'll even see an older men's liberation movement emerge. Tellingly, if you Google 'older men' today what comes up is Dating Older Men.

How does this help us in our own ageing? As with history, so with gender: the more we're able to understand how ageist assumptions shape our thoughts and behaviour, the less hold they'll have over us. If you recognize, for example, how far women are judged by their appearance and men by their vigour, you'll find it easier, as you leave your teens and twenties, to situate and challenge those stereotypes of the woman who's losing her looks and the man whose vigour is ebbing away. Let's not delude ourselves: this is the work of a lifetime. And it needs to be done in concert with others. But, as we begin to identify the caricatures and prejudices we've internalized and understand their social origins, they become more resistible. And this makes it possible to age more freely – to become more fully ourselves.

6. A Very Short Chapter on Death

Since 1951 no one in the USA has died of old age. This was the year old age was deleted as a cause of death from death certificates; from then on you could only die of a disease. In the UK doctors are advised to avoid 'old age' as the sole cause of death, except in very limited circumstances.

Such a change might seem benign: surely it helps us avoid seeing old age as the stepping stone to death? Shouldn't we applaud the idea that it's disease and not age that ends our life? But while this shift appears, on the face of it, simply to reflect advances in medical science, its causes and implications are more complex. Severing any link between ageing and death is another manifestation of our denial of death – death has to go underground, and not just literally. In addition, in both the USA and UK, it's now illegal to list 'natural causes' on its own on a death certificate: not only has this contributed to the medicalization of old age identified in Chapter 4, but it has also helped foment the view that death is unnatural.

Along with gerontophobia, our culture suffers from thanatophobia, an overwhelming fear of death. This is reinforced by the way that death, like old age, has been sequestered from the rest of society – more people now die in hospital or a nursing home than in their own home. Such is the taboo against death that children are often excluded from the funerals of relatives on the grounds that 'it will upset them', though they often later express regret that they had no opportunity to say goodbye.

The temerity to die

In Western countries death is increasingly regarded as medical failure rather than an inevitable part of life. There's just one entry for death in the index to Aubrey de Grey's 377-page book, *Ending Aging*. New Age guru Deepak Chopra invites his followers to become pioneers in a land where 'old age, senility, infirmity and death do not exist and are not even entertained as a possibility'. Now where would that be – la-la land? In highly individualistic cultures death seems like a personal affront, a narcissistic wound, an attack on our individual subjectivity. And this helps forge our attitudes to growing older.

Old age and death represent everything modern societies thought they'd vanquished and hoped they'd eliminated. Old people do something unforgiveable: by failing to control the eventual decline of their bodies, they contravene the idea that the human body is infinitely malleable. What a terrible reminder of our ultimate powerlessness, of the inevitability of death! For transgressing the idea of human omnipotence they must be punished and shamed – age-shamed. The more defended you are against your own mortality, the more likely you are to subscribe to ageist ideas: researchers have found, for example, that nursing staff with high levels of 'death anxiety' have significantly more negative attitudes to older people.

Admitting death

There is, though, another way of dealing with death that makes ageing much easier: paradoxically, it's thinking about our own mortality more and not less, and incorporating it into our daily lives. Death needs to accompany us through life, and not stalk us. Morbid? No – Buddhist.

Muriel Spark, although she was only 41 when her novel *Memento Mori* was published, understood this. All the book's elderly characters are plagued by anonymous phone-calls in which the caller only ever says the same solitary sentence, 'Remember you must die'. But, says Miss Taylor, one of the characters, it's difficult for people of 'advanced years' to start remembering that they might die. 'It is better to form the habit while young.' Another character, Henry Mortimer, goes further:

If I had my life over again I should form the habit of nightly composing myself to thoughts of death. I would practise, as it were, the remembrance of death. There is no other practice which so intensifies life. Death, when it approaches, ought not to take one by surprise. It should be part of the full expectancy of life. Without an ever-present sense of death life is insipid. You might as well live on the whites of eggs.

Practising remembering death: it's an intriguing idea and an eminently sensible one. The American poet May Sarton gave a lot of thought to the subject. As usual, she put it simply: 'One must live as though one were dying – and we all are, of course – because then the priorities become clear.'

Although she was only 41 when her novel *Memento Mori* was published, Muriel Spark understood the need for death to accompany us through life.

Coming to terms with our mortality isn't easily achieved, or a single event – it's a lifelong process. Of course death is frightening and can fill us with existential terror. As Woody Allen put it: 'I'm not afraid of death, I just don't want to be there when it happens.' Accepting death involves a kind of mourning – for oneself. It can also excite anger over the ways in which life has disappointed us, and we've disappointed others. (This is why it needs to begin early, so that we have enough time to make changes.) It demands a letting go of one's sense of omnipotence, a facing up to finitude. There's something humbling about it.

Although we all die in the singular, (our death, even if it happens in a war or plane crash, is particular to us), trying to accept it alongside others makes us feel less singled out, less persecuted by it. Interesting new initiatives are doing just this. At 'Death Cafe' events, people come together in a relaxed and safe setting to discuss death, drink tea and eat cake. They don't provide bereavement support or grief counselling; their objective is to 'increase awareness of death with a view to helping people make the most of their (finite) lives'. Some 1,000 people have participated so far in such cafes in the UK, USA, Canada, Australia and Italy.

Or there's the Order of the Good Death, founded in 2011 by Caitlin Doughty, a mortician and writer in Los Angeles, with the aim of bringing realistic discussion of death into popular culture. With her interest in bodily decomposition, Doughty might seem to lie at the fetishistic end of the spectrum. But less esoteric is her idea of making death a part of life by staring down one's fears. Comments on the Order of the Good Death's website show that there's a real appetite for opening up death in this way.

Maggie Kuhn used to encourage people to compile a life line or life review from their birth. When she urged them to also put in the year they thought they'd die, people always gasped. She maintained, though, that this helped raise their consciousness of their own death. For once you start to really take on board the fact that you're going to die, old age becomes a lot less terrifying: it means you're not dead yet.

'People who cannot look ahead as they grow older *back* into the future,' according to Rabbi Zalman Schachter-Shalomi, so all they see is the past. But 'when we de-repress the fear of death, we reclaim the energy that has gone into denial. We feel buoyed up as streams of creative energy course through our bodies, minds and nervous systems. By facing a subject that usually depresses and terrifies us, we feel lighter, freer, more perceptually and cognitively alive in all our encounters.'

This is an essential task for the non-old for another reason too. The more that we engage with death when it isn't imminent, the less we'll require of older people that they be associated only with dying. Old age will no longer be a synonym for death, or dying, but for living.

And when reach their age we'll reap the benefits.

7. Arc of Life

'Symmetry', a TV ad for Marie Curie Cancer Care, attracted almost universal praise when it was launched in 2013. It intercut moving scenes of a baby's first steps, first birthday, first shave, first awkward teenage kiss, with last experiences – a couple's last tender touch, a last shave, a last kiss. The caption read: 'Your last moments should mean as much as your first.' Part of an appeal to raise money for good end-of-life care, the ad was seen as an admirable contribution to breaking the taboos around death.

But it was also innovative in another, less obvious way: it showed an entire human lifespan. As its director Tom Tagholm pointed out, 'It is putting death into a different context, the context of life.'

Contrast this with an exhibit at the Boston Museum of Science in 2000. In a booth open only to children under 15, participants had their photo taken and then, at the press of a button, a simulation appeared, showing what they'd look like at yearly intervals until the age of 69. The computer added grotesque pouches and blotches, elongated and sagged their faces and gave them heavily rutted lines. The boys lost their hair. No one looked good, reported the cultural critic Margaret Morganroth Gullette, let alone humorous, contented or beautiful – the software engineers had based the algorithm on 'older equals uglier'. No wonder the children emerged shaken, saying 'I don't want to grow old.'

The Boston exhibit embodied a whole set of entrenched cultural beliefs that prevent us from seeing our lives as a single, finite entity. It estranged the children from their future selves, encouraging in them instead the desire to freeze it at one particular age. Welcome to the world of anti-ageing: for, as these children grow, they'll encounter many more reasons to fear their own ageing, making it even harder for them to conceive of their life as an entity.

Life as a whole

The concept of a lifespan or life cycle is becoming increasingly alien to us. Yet the psychoanalyst Erik Erikson, who identified eight stages of psychosocial development from infancy to late adulthood, regarded each one of them as crucial. 'As we come to the last stage [old age], we become aware of the fact that our civilization really does not harbour a concept of the whole of life.'

The final stage, Erikson maintained, offers us the opportunity to establish an integrated self, to draw on the sustenance of the past (good memories, experiences and achievements) while still retaining a vital involvement in the present. It gives us the chance to see our life as a whole, to come to terms with its meaning, purpose and shape, instead of thinking of it as a series of discrete, atomized stages.

There's an important reason for reconceiving our life in this way *before we reach old age*. Connecting with our future self allows us to develop earlier on the resources that will serve us best later – resources like the ability to make new friends when we lose old ones, to accept help graciously, to value internal resources at least as much as external ones, and to be able to let go. Without this earlier work, we have to face old age bereft of the capacities necessary to flourish in those years, when they're harder (though not impossible) to develop.

The values most admired by advanced industrial societies and the market – a single-minded focus on productivity – are precisely those of least help with ageing. People who live their earlier lives as if they're never going to age often find retirement and the loss of a professional identity particularly traumatic: they've failed to cultivate those qualities that can endure, and without the containing structure imposed by work, even if they complained about it at the time, they're at a loss.

Our younger self

There's another compelling reason for re-establishing the link between our younger and older selves: because they're so viscerally enmeshed. Poor nutrition in early childhood, for instance, has been linked to high blood pressure in old age. In addition, researchers at King's College London have found that twenty-two molecules already present when we're born are linked to our health in old age. And emotional resilience as we age is related to our earliest experiences of being cared for. Such vivid connections, physiological and psychological, between the two ends of life – and of course everything that lies in between.

Although we live in a Peter Pan culture where youth is the yardstick, young people need to be re-imagined, too, since they're also harmed by ageist ideas and even by age-resistance. Idealizing youth at the expense of age, for instance, conceals how hard it often is to be young. (And when young people don't live up to our unattainable vision of them – as of course they can't – they're then demonized as 'feral'.) Youth and age get polarized and the years in between stereotyped ('middle-aged' is rife with connotations, most of them undesirable). This distorts the fact that flux and change are inevitable throughout the life course.

Our future selves

One way of widening our vision so that it includes the entire lifespan is by identifying with older people. And no one has described this more beautifully than Henri Nouwen. Nouwen viewed ageing as one of the most essential human processes, one that could be denied only with great harm. In a slim co-written volume called *Aging: The Fulfillment of Life*, first published in 1974, the Dutch-born Catholic priest urges us to break through the artificial boundaries between the generations. We must resist the temptation to make ageing into the problem of old people, he argues passionately, because it's a way of denying that that we too are implicated in the process. Instead he wants us 'to allow the elderly to cure us of our separatist tendencies and bring us into a closer and more intimate contact with our own ageing.'

In an ageist culture this is no easy task. But to care for the ageing, he insists, we need to 'make ourselves available to the experience of becoming old . . . [to allow] an old man or woman to come alive in the center of our own existence.' This is a profound act of empathy and humanity, and can open the door to a powerful emotional maturing and growth. But we can't take the step if we feel the need to disavow old people because they remind us of our own mortality.

Disowning weakness

Another way of making the ageing process less frightening is by reclaiming some of the feelings of fragility that we've offloaded onto old people. This is one of the most important psychological mechanisms through which most of us protect ourselves from the knowledge that all of us are ageing, all of us will die and none of us is invincible. We disown the feelings of weakness and vulnerability that arise at every stage of life, youth included, and transfer them instead into older people. With such a heavy load of fragility to bear – their own and that belonging to the rest of us – no wonder they're always shown with walking-sticks and Zimmer frames. Who could walk energetically and upright carrying such cargo?

Oscar Wilde created the most brilliant and graphic example of this sort of psychological 'splitting' in *The Picture of Dorian Gray*: here the portrait has to suffer all the visible signs of ageing that the narcissistic young man who was its sitter can't tolerate.

Projection like this is a cause of elder abuse: the despised part of the self is split off, attributed to someone else and can then be damaged without, apparently, hurting oneself. Splitting has also been enacted physically: Germany is now 'exporting' – some call it 'deporting' – thousands of old and sick Germans to retirement and rehabilitation centres in Eastern Europe and Asia because it's cheaper. This is 'disowning' old people literally.

It's not hard to see why it arises. Powerlessness is perhaps the hardest state for us to tolerate today. Our culture speaks approvingly (and often helpfully) about 'empowerment'. In the process, though, we neglect the importance of learning to accept limitation and weakness, incapacity and dependency, yet no one can go their entire life without experiencing them.

The age deniers displace the painful losses and limitations that can come with chronic illness and disability from the third age onto the fourth age, so that they can safely be ignored for longer. But piling all vulnerability into the last years makes ageing much more frightening. Old people 'carry' a burden for the not-yet-old – all fragility is invested in them so that the rest of us don't need to feel it. And yet they are the ones who are made to feel burdensome.

Interdependent

But a growing number of thinkers have found a much more radical and exciting way of thinking about vulnerability: they're challenging our conventional understandings of the meaning of dependency. American activist Barbara Macdonald was one of the first to re-examine her own assumptions about physical strength and weakness. It started on a march in New England in 1978 when she was 65. One of the marshals tasked with keeping the march moving, seeing Macdonald's grey hair and wrinkles, told her that if she couldn't keep up she should move to another part of the line. At first Macdonald was shocked and upset. Then, though, she struggled with herself, reasoning that there was nothing wrong with being physically weak:

'If it does not happen to be true of me now, it will be true of me soon. If I have pride in my strength now, it is false pride and . . . I [will] feel shame in my lack of strength later.'

The Gray Panthers went further, rejecting the false opposition between independence and dependence, and championing the idea of *interdependence* instead. As Maggie Kuhn explained:

> We say that we cannot be human all by ourselves; we need each other. I have arthritis and I have failing vision and the two conditions . . . complicate my life . . . I say to people: 'Help me, may I take your hand up this step or down this kerb.' I have learnt not to feel diminished by asking for help. Instead, I feel a new kind of reward from human love: I touch your arm and something happens, something that is warming and affirming.

Some people are better at this than others. Psychotherapist Marie de Hennezel has observed many older people entrusting their body to other people's care with grace, and without embarrassment or humiliation. It's as if they help their carers look after them.

Most recently, American anthropologist Mary Catherine Bateson has urged us to see both giving and taking as part of a single pattern and not as alternatives. In America, she argues, there's so much stigma attached to needing help that it's easy to despise those who do. But when economists talk of 'dependency ratios' – of young people working to support older people – they're obscuring the real reciprocity on which all human relationships depend. Because of course there's exchange in each direction in every human activity. Doesn't the doctor need their patients, and learn from them? And surely the comedian depends on the audience?

So how does this help us deal with our fears about growing older? Taking back our anxieties about the precariousness and vulnerability that are part of the human condition but which we've offloaded onto elderly people, and learning to tolerate dependence rather than locating all our fears about it in older people – what a kind gesture to make to our future ageing self! This frees us to re-imagine old people, and identify them not purely with death and disability but also with long life. It enables us to realize that growth and psychological development aren't a property of our earliest years but can continue throughout the life cycle.

Losing and gaining

Among the other states that need to be cultivated in preparation for old age, as well as during it, are mourning and gratitude. Old age, says Erikson, is a time of relinquishing – friends, old roles, even possessions that belonged to earlier stages of life. Yet at every stage of life some attachments need to be given up for others to develop, in order to move forward. Such losses and endings are a kind of bereavement, and are bound to recur throughout our lives, especially at periods of greatest transition. We need to acknowledge and mourn them if they're not to impede change. This is one of the 'developmental tasks' of ageing, at every age.

The Italian film director Bernardo Bertolucci had a fall in Rome in his sixties; failed surgery left him unable to walk. He assumed that he'd never direct another film, but 'everything changed the moment I accepted the situation.' He realized that 'he could be happy even here', in his wheelchair. His most recent film was released in 2013, when he was 73.

Mourning creates a space in which a sense of gratitude can develop – gratitude for what remains, or for what unfolds in place of what's been lost. This ability to be thankful, about small things as well as major ones, has to be cultivated if it doesn't come naturally. We may mock those forever praising 'a nice cup of tea', or who, when they go to bed at night, look back on their day in search of things to be grateful about. It may feel a little mechanical but, if practised regularly, learning to appreciate small gestures, tiny pieces of good fortune and, equally, the lack of bad things becomes a very valuable habit indeed.

The indomitable playwright and analyst Florida Scott-Maxwell had this habit in abundance. Her unvarnished account of being old, *The Measure of My Days*, is full of rage, passion and insight. Infirmity is there, certainly, but it isn't the pivot of her existence. And the absence of pain becomes a cause for elation: 'This morning when I woke and knew that I had had a fair night, that my pains were not too bad, I lay waiting for the uplifting moment when I pull back the curtains, see the sky, and I surprised myself by saying out loud: "My dear, dear days."'

The radical old

In English 'old' is the opposite of 'young' but also of 'new'. This identifies elderly people with everything that's conservative. What a calumny!

Maggie Kuhn saw older people in precisely the opposite way. In the vanguard of social change, they're society's futurists – testing out new instruments, technologies, ideas and styles of living. Older people, she insisted, were ideally placed to be watchdogs of public bodies, guardians of the public interest and common good, advocates of consumers' rights, whistle-blowers and monitors of corporate power. They weren't just custodians of the past but also trustees of the future. This is a very different image from that of disengaged, withdrawn individual that we're usually presented with whenever old age is depicted.

'Why should I care about posterity?' Groucho Marx famously quipped. 'What's posterity ever done for me?' But older people are increasingly busying themselves with posterity, wanting to leave behind a more sustainable planet. And of course they're particularly well placed for this task: because they remember what delayed gratification feels like, and their experience has taught them that life can be comfortable and entertaining without excessive consumption. Those who lived through the Second World War also remember how to make Mock Plum Pudding or Imitation Eggs, and will never forget the taste of a banana when it was a rare, prized jewel.

If we're prepared to look at age without prejudice we may be heartened by what we find. We routinely hear about old people as recipients of care; what gets passed over is that they're also massive providers of it. According to the National Citizenship Survey, 30 per cent of 65- to 74-years-olds volunteer regularly, as do one-fifth of people 75 and over. Volunteering bridges the divide between old people receiving welfare and dispensing it: it enables them to tackle other people's social exclusion or isolation at the same time as their own. What's particularly exciting is a growing recognition among voluntary organizations that even frail older people and those with significant disabilities can, with enough flexibility, be recruited and retained as volunteers.

Older people's reduced energy seems to be more than compensated for by the increased amount of time they have available. A report by the think tank ResPublica in 2011 found that, when it came to civil activism – acting as local councillors, school governors or magistrates – people over 75 were as active as 26- to 34-year-olds. One reason that old people give for volunteering is personal growth – yes, even at 90. Ageing like this doesn't seem quite so bad.

The fear of dementia

Until, that is, you notice Alzheimer's lurking in the shadows, waiting to derail any optimistic discussion. Dementia seems to have become the emblem of old age, even though it isn't caused by ageing, and isn't an inevitable part of the ageing process. At its worst, its effects are devastating. Yet the myths – that it obliterates all memory, and that people with Alzheimer's can't learn anything new – erase not only the past of people with dementia but also their future. In fact, though their cognitive and complex memories are compromised, their bodily, emotional, skill and artistic memories are often still intact and acute.

Many different exciting new projects are now stimulating these other faculties. Like Artists for Alzheimer's, through which artists share their work with people with dementia. They also organize tours of museums, such as the Museum of Modern Art in New York and the Louvre in Paris: here people with dementia show not only a remarkable sensitivity to the work of others but also do powerful creative work themselves.

In Music for Life's interactive music workshops in care homes and day centres, professional musicians improvise alongside people with dementia. Other projects have created books of startling poems out of the conversations of people with dementia: they speak in metaphors, a highly lyrical language of elation, wit and despair. Projects like York Dementia Without Walls are developing the concept of dementia-friendly cities, on the grounds that what's good for people with dementia is good for everybody. Extraordinarily, there's even evidence that psychoanalysis can help develop some peace of mind in both people with dementia and those looking after them.

What these projects also do is bring people of all ages and life stages together, and remind us of our shared humanity – and fragility.

Ageing contentedly

Alzheimer's affects large numbers, but they're still a minority of old people. The majority of older people without brain disease maintain a sense of reasonable wellbeing until just before they die, according to three major American studies. They're also less depressed than the general population, and most aren't incapacitated by illness. Instead, the Harvard Study of Adult Development found the majority constantly reinvent their lives and don't lose sight of why they wanted to keep on living. Even if they fall ill, their reaction to their condition is more important than their objective state of health.

Ageing inevitably brings losses and usually some physical deterioration, but those who remain engaged with life manage to maintain a positive ratio of enthusiasm to resignation. The ones who fare best not only care about what they leave behind for the next generation, but are also able to keep learning from people both older and younger than themselves.

This isn't old age as we've been taught to fear it. It's more like W. B. Yeats's characterization of it in 'Sailing to Byzantium':

> An aged man is but a paltry thing,
> A tattered coat upon a stick, unless
> Soul clap its hands and sing . . .

How can we encourage our soul to sing? Perhaps by realizing that souls need nurturing at every age, and that we need to begin the process long before we reach old age. If we can draw sustenance from these alternative views of ageing while also directly facing our anxieties, if we're able to give ourselves permission to grow older but at the same time resist the myths about ageing, then the gift we receive in return is invaluable: the ability to position ourselves in a whole lifespan, and see the integrity of a human life, however long or short it might be.

Those who urge us to fight ageing are, in effect, inviting us to stop growing and developing. In so doing, they're depriving us of the opportunity to carry out and successfully complete the task of being alive and human. Individually and collectively we're being infantilized: we should insist on the right to grow up.

Growing older, many believe, can be taught. Certainly we have to teach children that they won't always be young: education and debate can encourage them to imagine themselves at each stage in the life cycle – neither decrepit nor omnipotent. This in itself will help foster a sense of identification with people of every age, older ones included. Some of the ways that this can be done haven't yet been dreamed up, but as more and more people anticipate longevity and engage with the life cycle – prospectively and not only retrospectively – all sorts of innovative projects and communities will emerge to help us sustain Erikson's 'vital engagement' throughout the lifespan, and not just in the earliest stages.

And maybe someone will design a photo booth that allows children to project themselves forward into fully rounded, witty, attractive and contented people – at every age.

Conclusion

How's Gina getting on? Rather better than when we last saw her. As it happens she's been reading this book: someone gave it to her as a thirtieth birthday present. Under plain cover. She knows that books don't change lives (only authors think they do – and only before they start writing), but they can fertilize new ideas and she's been having some, mainly because of the recent death of her grandmother.

Betty was 91 when she died. She was a vibrant woman, elegant to the last, who became less judgemental as she aged and not more.

Gina loved her, and at her funeral made three resolutions:

1. Never again to say of someone 'she must have been beautiful', as though age were some necrotizing organism that eats away at beauty.

2. Whenever she felt anxious about her own encroaching wrinkles, to imagine herself fifteen years older so that, in comparison, she looked positively peachy. She thought of this as a reverse facelift. ('But what will you do,' demanded her mother, 'when you reach 90?' 'By then I'll be happy just to still be alive.')

3. To remember that Betty, until the very end, thought that life was an adventure: she was always seizing new opportunities, conversing with strangers and reading new books. (She was enthralled by the e-reader Gina gave her, which, by magnifying

the font of downloaded books, gave her access to a vast library at a stroke, despite her failing sight.)

Although her life had been extremely hard at times and she was no stranger to anxiety and loss, Betty was committed to living, and consciously made decisions that sided with life. She showed Gina that ageing can mean *adding* new resources and qualities as you grow older, and not *subtracting* them. Gina is also coming to realize that growing older is a privilege which, instead of fearing, she might do better to hope for. (*Hope I age* – what a slogan this would be!) In short, she has started to understand that ageing is a process, and not a crisis.

There's never been a better time to age. This might sound like a curious claim, after the inventory of gerontophobia, prejudice and discrimination laid out on some of the previous pages. But there's never been a better time to challenge the narratives of decline and age-resistance, and seek out other people in the growing age-acceptance movement – those who are pro-age.

Of course the conditions that make ageing hard in modern societies need collective social and political action, but there are campaigns on everything from continuing education to the provision of public toilets. And there are so many more that need starting or strengthening – support, training and decent pay for carers, for instance. Or the right for old people to remain embodied: as much as younger people, older people need to touch and be touched; to taste good food; to stretch, move and dance.

Perhaps we should revive the Age Awareness Training courses developed by Catherine Itzin in the 1980s. These allowed people to 'own' their age, to think in a safe group about what's good about the age they are, and to discuss their fears of ageing and hopes for their future aged selves.

Above all, we need to remind ourselves that ageing is a lifelong process, and not just something that occurs at the end of our lives: the seeds we plant earlier are what we harvest later. Mary Catherine Bateson has suggested that, today, 'we live longer but think shorter.' So we need to adjust our thinking, both individually and collectively: to both live *and* think longer. It's easy to get dispirited along the way, to feel that the forces ranged against ageing in the full, free and creative sense discussed here are too powerful. But apartheid and the Berlin Wall also used to seem as if they'd last forever. Eventually, though, both were dismantled. Eventually, too, we may come to view both ageism and the denial of age as enduring but now discredited historical relics. The trick is to live our lives as though that time had already arrived.

This book asks you to try to reconceive your own ageing, and to get in touch with it. It even has the temerity to suggest that, instead of fearing or denying the ageing process, it can be embraced. It argues that we can become more vital and not less as we grow older. In order to reach this place, though, some hard psychic work is required: vulnerability and death both need to be granted entry and not magicked away. Acknowledging death graces us with a sense of perspective: it reminds us that we have only a finite number of breaths; it makes us ask ourselves 'How will I feel when I get to the end of my life having done/without having done this?'

We also have to think in terms of our whole lifespan, and not mentally lop off those ages that we dread, in a kind of manic 'present-ism'. On the contrary, it's through accepting that life is

An Ali Winstanley photograph: We can become more, not less, vital as we grow older.

finite, through developing the courage to meet the inevitable losses we encounter face-on, that we acquire the greatest capacity for vitality and enjoyment of the present.

How to age? We become more different as we age, and not less; we all flourish at different ages. For instance Maxine, of the older women's network the Hen Co-op, noticed that

> Other people sometimes seem embarrassed when I say I'm old. They're quick to reassure me that I'm not *really* old, as if it were some horrible disfigurement, or a disease they're worried about catching . . . [but] I am 63 years old and for the first time in my life, I feel that my age fits me. Or I fit my age. It hasn't always been so.

To fit your age is a marvellous concept, a sign of real growth. Maxine is able to see her age through her own experience, and not through other people's stereotype of what it means or should mean. It's rare to hear someone claim their age like this, and live it.

Of course there are no recipes for 'ageing well'. (It's also a double-edged term, because it brings with it the somewhat alarming possibility of 'ageing badly', whatever this might mean. Dying?) Yet this hasn't stopped many people trying to work out what it means to age well.

For the novelist Edith Wharton it was being 'unafraid of change, insatiable in intellectual curiosity, interested in big things, and happy in small ways.'

The cellist Pablo Casals, when asked by one of his pupils why, at the age of 91, he continued to practise, replied, 'Because I am making progress.'

Florida Scott-Maxwell, meanwhile, had a typically robust view. 'I want to tell people approaching and perhaps fearing age that it is a time of discovery. If they say – "Of what?" I can only answer, "We must each find out for ourselves, otherwise it won't be discovery."'

How to age? You reach the final pages of a supposedly self-help book, and all it tells you is that you've got to work it out for yourself . . .

All right then: the best way of 'ageing well' turns out to be the same as 'living well'.

When a Zen master was dying, his disciples scoured the Tokyo cake shops for his favourite pastry. Though he was weak he munched his way through it happily. As his energy waned, his followers leaned in and asked if he had any final words of instruction for them. 'Yes,' he replied with his last breath, 'this cake is delicious.'

May our cakes be delicious too.

Homework

Introduction

Simone de Beauvoir's tour-de-force, *Old Age* (Penguin, 1977), was criticized when it was first published for its supposedly bleak view of ageing, but is packed with fascinating detail and her customary insight. If only for supplying us with the brilliantly pithy phrase 'Aged by Culture', Margaret Morganroth Gullette's book of that title (University of Chicago Press, 2004) would be worth perusing, but it's also wide-ranging and thoughtful, a pioneering contribution to 'age studies'.

1. What is Age?

Savour some of the inspiring personal accounts of growing older: May Sarton's *At Seventy* (W. W. Norton & Co., 1993), Maggie Kuhn's autobiography *No Stone Unturned* (Ballantine, 1991), the exuberant Florida Scott-Maxwell with *The Measure of My Days* (Penguin, 1979) and the Hen Co-op's *Growing Old Disgracefully* (Piatkus, 1993), where some of the inspiring case-histories included here come from. Diana Athill's *Somewhere Towards The End* (Granta, 2008) observes the process of getting older with admirable cool-headedness.

2. Fear of Ageing

Christopher Phillipson's *Ageing* (Polity Press, 2013), and Phil Mullan, in *The Imaginary Time Bomb: Why an Ageing Population is Not a Social Problem* (I. B. Tauris, 2002), dismantle the arguments about a coming 'silver tsunami' of sickly older dependents. There's a wealth of illuminating essays in *Images of Aging: Cultural Representations of Later Life*, edited by Mike Featherstone and Andrew Wernick (Routledge, 1995).

A generation of brilliant British social and cultural gerontologists have provided a language in which to analyse the fourth age. Anything by Chris Gilleard, Paul Higgs, Ian Rees Jones, Julia Twigg and Bill Bytheway is illuminating.

Take a look, too, at www.yoisthisageist.com, where you can post examples of ageist comments seen and heard: it's part of Ashton Applewhite's 'This Chair Rocks' blog. And watch Billy Wilder's film *Sunset Boulevard* (1950), with Gloria Swanson's fabulous over-the-top performance, its most famous line 'I'm still big – it's the pictures that got small'.

3. Embracing Age

George E. Vaillant's *Aging Well* (Little, Brown, 2003) is full of fascinating life-histories showing how people have overcome or transformed their early experiences. Zalman Schachter-Shalomi's *From Age-ing to Sage-ing* (Grand Central Publishing, 1998) is as New Age as it title suggests, but still uplifting: the story of the Zen master in my Conclusion comes from here. The Worsthorne quote comes from John Burningham's splendid anthology *The Time of Your Life* (Bloomsbury, 2003). The French psychotherapist Marie de Hennezel's passionate meditation on how to maintain vitality in old age is evident from the title of her best-seller, *The Warmth of the Heart Prevents Your Body From Rusting* (PanMacmillan, 2012), even if she lapses into the serenity stereotype by the end. In *Growing Old: a Journey of Self-discovery* (Routledge, 2009), psychoanalyst Danielle Quinodoz recounts, movingly, how her elderly patients managed to repair emotional wounds they suffered earlier in their lives.

4. Between the Ages

Fascinating historical accounts of ageing are found in Thomas Cole's *The Journey of Life* (Cambridge University Press, 1992) and David Hackett Fischer's *Growing Old in America* (Oxford University Press, 1978). *The Long History of Old Age*, edited by Pat Thane (Thames & Hudson, 2005), is wide-ranging and sumptuously illustrated, while Richard Sennett is an indispensable guide to the deep impact of *The Culture of the New Capitalism* (Yale University Press, 2007).

Betty Friedan provides a caustic view of America's age-segregation in *The Fountain of Age* (Jonathan Cape, 1993). The description of the female geriatric ward in a nursing home in Muriel Spark's novel *Memento Mori* (Virago, 2010), where everyone is called Granny even if they're not one, evokes ageing more effectively than any treatise, but Cicero's *De Senectute* is still eloquent (W. Heinemann, 1989).

5. Age and Gender

Kick off with Susan Sontag's seminal essay 'The double standard of aging' (*Saturday Review*, 23 September, 1972), and follow it with Julia Twigg's revealing *Fashion and Age* (Bloomsbury Academic, 2013). Elissa Melamed, in her pioneering *Mirror Mirror: The Terror of Not Being Young* (Simon & Schuster, 1983), bursts with insight about images of older women. See too the new Charter Against Ageism and Sexism in the Media: www.newdynamics.group.shef.ac.uk/petition.html. www.growingolddisgracefully.org.uk is probably the oldest British blog for older women.

6. A Very Short Chapter on Death

Muriel Spark again. And Michael Haneke's luminous film *Amour* (2012).

7. Arc of Life

Henri Neuwen and Walter Gaffney's small book *Aging: The Fulfillment of Life* (Doubleday, 1986) takes less than an hour to read – half of it is made up of photographs – but its shining humanity lingers for a long time after (and you don't need to be a believer, as Neuwen was, to feel it).

Acknowledgements

This may be a slim volume but its gestation was long. Caroline Pick, Barbara Rosenbaum and Lennie Goodings have been constantly encouraging, as has my agent, the indefatigable Natasha Fairweather of AP Watt at United Agents. Gianna Williams helped me understand the subject in a different way. My thanks to Juliette Mitchell and The School of Life for their enthusiastic response to the book, to Cindy Chan at Pan Macmillan for her sensitive editing, and to Will Atkins for his splendid copy-editing. My long-standing interest in ageing was inspired by my parents, Josef and Natalia, who were blessed with longevity: their vitality didn't diminish in their nineties, my pianist mother giving her last concert at 94. My daughters, Bianca and Lola, have graciously tolerated my preoccupation with the subject of ageing; Bianca also supplied me with valuable links and suggestions for reading. Peter Lewis nourished me and made me laugh through the research and writing. He personifies the way that energy, curiosity and a passionate engagement with life can grow with age.

Picture Acknowledgements

The author and publisher would like to thank the following for permission to reproduce the images used in this book:

Page 5 Guggenheim Museum © Adam Eastland / Getty Images

Page 11 Maggie Kuhn in 1981 © Mickey Adair / Getty Images

Page 17 Brad Pitt in *The Curious Case of Benjamin Button*, 2008 © REX / Snap Stills

Page 19 Salad making, c.1955 © FPG / Hulton Archive / Getty Images

Page 28 Child Beauty Pageant © Evan Hurd / Sygma / Corbis

Page 33 Stitched drawing © Georgie Meadows

Page 35 Gloria Swanson in *Sunset Boulevard* © J. R. Eyerman / Time & Life Pictures / Getty Images

Page 37 *Portrait of the artist's mother*, 1514 (charcoal on paper), Dürer or Duerer, Albrecht (1471–1528) © Kupferstichkabinett, Berlin, Germany / Giraudon / The Bridgeman Art Library

Page 57 Bud Cort and Ruth Gordon in *Harold and Maude*, 1971 © Snap Stills / REX

Page 62 *I Am Still Learning* (*Aun Aprendo*) (charcoal on paper), Goya y Lucientes, Francisco Jose de (1746–1828) © Prado, Madrid, Spain / The Bridgeman Art Library

Page 67 Senior woman wearing a feather boa © Cohen / Ostrow / Getty Images

Page 76 Portrait of William Hiseland, 1750 (oil on canvas), Alsop, George, (fl.1722–30) © Royal Hospital Chelsea, London, UK / The Stapleton Collection / The Bridgeman Art Library

Page 80 Margot Smyly in 1977 © REX / Peter Akehurst / Associated Newspapers

Page 82 Anne Bancroft and Murray Hamilton in *The Graduate*, 1967 © c.Everett Collection / REX

Page 95 Maitri House, an intergenerational group home © Katherine Frey / The Washington Post / Getty Images

Page 101 Young woman and hands of an old woman © G. Baden / Corbis

Page 107 Paul Newman © DMI / Time & Life Pictures / Getty Images

Page 120 Muriel Spark at work, 1960 © Evening Standard / Hulton Archive / Getty Images

Page 140 Nancy © Ali Winstanley

Notes

TOOLS FOR THINKING

A NEW RANGE OF NOTEBOOKS, PENCILS, CARDS
& GIFTS FROM THE SCHOOL OF LIFE

Good thinking requires good tools. To complement our classes, books and therapies, THE SCHOOL OF LIFE now offers a range of stationery products and gifts that are both highly useful and stimulating for the eye and mind.

If you enjoyed this book, we'd encourage you to check out other titles in the series:

Other series from The School of Life:

Life Lessons from Great Thinkers:
Bergson, Byron, Freud, Hobbes, Kierkegaard, Nietzsche

If you'd like to explore more good ideas for everyday life, The School of Life runs a regular programme of classes, weekends, secular sermons and events in London and other cities around the world.

Browse our shop and visit:

THESCHOOLOFLIFE.COM
TWITTER.COM/THESCHOOLOFLIFE

panmacmillan.com
twitter.com/panmacmillan